To Pame'
Hope :

GHOST HUNTER
True-Life Encounters from the North East

by

Darren W. Ritson

**Grosvenor House
Publishing Limited**

This book is published by
Grosvenor House Publishing Ltd
28-30 High Street, Guildford, Surrey, GU1 3HY.
www.grosvenorhousepublishing.co.uk

A CIP record for this book
is available from the British Library

ISBN 1-905529-75-9

*I WOULD LIKE TO DEDICATE THIS BOOK
TO THE MEMORY OF HARRY PRICE (1881-1948),
TO MY PARTNER OF 11 YEARS JAYNE WATSON,
TO OUR DAUGHTER ABBEY MAY RITSON
WHO WAS BORN ON 1st MAY 2006,
AND TO MY MOTHER AND FATHER*

Acknowledgments

First let me begin by thanking all The North East Ghost In-Spectres investigation team members past and present. Present members include Suzanne McKay, Glenn Hall, Claire Smith, Darren Olley, Julie Olley, Mark Winter, John Maltman and Fiona Vipond.

I would also like to thank Drew Bartley, Fiona Vipond, Lee Stephenson and Suzanne McKay of the G.H.O.S.T Investigation team and Cindy Nunn and Colin Nunn from A.P.I (Anomalous Phenomena Investigations) for inviting me to the investigations that have been reported herein.

I am indebted to Mike Hallowell (The North East Ghost In-Spectres team patron) for his endless help, support and guidance, and the publicity he has given me during the course of the compilation of this book. I would also like to thank Tony Liddell Bsc (Founder of Otherworld North East) for the advice he has also given me along the way. Without their help this book would have taken twice as long to complete.

To all the guest investigators that have attended our investigations and offered your support I give you my sincere thanks. You know who you are!

My thanks go to all the custodians, managers, and property-owners that have allowed our team access to their properties and locations for our research. These include Gladys Parker from Byker Community Centre, Corrina Orde and all the staff at The Schooner Hotel, Alan Milburn from Bowes Railway Museum, Alex Croom from Tyne and Wear Museums, the anonymous owners of "the pub" in Cumbria, Sue Birkbeck from The Marsden Grotto pub, Paul McDonald from the society of antiquities in Newcastle upon Tyne, Karl Edmondson, Owner of the haunted cockpit, James and Lisa McLeod from Harperley Prisoner of War Camp, Pat, Bruno and Linda from the Manor House in County Durham, Jo Bean from the El-Coto restaurant Newcastle, the manager and owners from El-Torero restaurant Newcastle, Chris Armstrong from Sea Nightclub and everyone one else who has played a part in allowing our team in to investigate their premises. Without your consent, this book would never have been written.

I would also like to thank the late Harry Price (1881 – 1948), and Peter Underwood for all the motivation you have given me through your writing. Your books are inspirational.

Thanks to Cindy Nunn from API for the help with the El-Coto Chapter and for the use of the POW photo. © Cindy and Colin Nunn.

A Massive thank you goes to Jayne Watson for her patience, understanding and the support she has given me while writing this book. I love you.

Front cover design and photographs by Darren W Ritson.

Front cover constructed by Michael Hallowell, Thunderbird craft and media.

Images

Contents

Foreword   ix

Introduction   xi

CHAPTER 1.   What is a ghost?   1

CHAPTER 2.   My Interest in the paranormal.   9

CHAPTER 3.   A tribute to Harry Price.   15

CHAPTER 4.   The orb and light anomaly phenomenon.   21

CHAPTER 5.   Ghost hunting equipment.   27

CHAPTER 6.   The community spirit.   35

CHAPTER 7.   Wall-to-Wall activity.   41

CHAPTER 8.   Train of thoughts.   47

CHAPTER 9.   Roman ghosts.   55

CHAPTER 10.   G.H.O.S.T in the pub.   63

CHAPTER 11.   A touch of spirit.   69

CHAPTER 12.   To keep vigil.   95

CHAPTER 13.   Plane old ghosts.   101

CHAPTER 14.   Eternally captive.   107

CHAPTER 15.   Kids will be kids.   113

CHAPTER 16.   Serving up some spirit.   119

Contents

CHAPTER 17.   Serving up some spirit. Part 2   127

CHAPTER 18.   The mystery of the morgue.   133

CHAPTER 19.   One for the children,
               a charity investigation.   139

CHAPTER 20.   Can you help me?   147

Afterword   155

Glossary of terms   159

About the Author   163

Foreword

I have known Darren Ritson for many years. We're both in the same game, you see; the game of ghost-hunting.

Oh, when I call it a "game" I don't mean to infer that we don't take our craft seriously. We most certainly do. But, like a big game hunter, we enjoy the thrill of the chase. Darren and I can smell a ghost in a medieval castle as easily as a good ol' country boy can smell a bear in the woods, mark my words.

Mind you, the tools of the trade are a little different. Game hunters use shotguns. In our experience these usually prove remarkably ineffective when chasing denizens of the spirit world, but give us an EMF meter or a digital thermometer and we'll bag you a brace of poltergeists before sun-up, no worries.

Seriously though, ghost-hunting is not a hobby or a pastime. At least, it shouldn't be. Ghost-hunters like Darren and I enjoy our work, but we're never frivolous about it. There really are insubstantial entities out there that seem to inhabit a quasi-real world which we can sometimes see but rarely, if ever, touch. In this volume you'll read Darren Ritson's own, first-hand account of how he tries to uncover the truth about wraiths, apparitions and ghosts on a weekly basis.

I have to be honest and say that there are a lot of "wannabes" in our chosen field of endeavour. I have seen supposed ghost-hunters dress up in gaudy cloaks and wave exotic swords around like a bit-part actor from Conan the Barbarian. I have seen others "tooled up" with so many bits of useless equipment that they could hardly walk let alone chase the shades of the dead through the corridors of a haunted inn. Real ghost-hunters don't go on like this.

Real ghost-hunters, like Darren, study the form like a good gambler. They don't have all the answers, but they're dedicated enough to keep searching for them. Real ghost-hunters will admit to being scared. After all, we're dealing with the unknown here.

There is no philosophy in Darren's book. If he doesn't know he doesn't pretend to know. He simply relates the facts. The strength of Ghost Hunter is that it is an unvarnished peek into a world that very few people know anything about. Ghost Hunter contains no flim-flam, no exotically-clad super psychics screaming their heads off every time a floorboard creaks. This is ghost-hunting as it really is.

Please don't – or rather do – have nightmares....

Mike Hallowell

Mike Hallowell is a full time author and broadcaster who runs his own media business. He has studied and written about the paranormal for nearly forty years and pens the country's longest-running column in a provincial newspaper dealing with the subject.

Introduction

They say everyone is born with psychic powers or abilities, and when most people grow up to adulthood they have forgotten how to use them. As the mind is clouded by society, and the more we cram into our heads as we learn and mature, I believe that part of our brain (the subconscious mind) loses what I would consider to be the ultimate faculty.

Have you ever thought about phoning a friend you have not been in contact with for a while, and on approaching the telephone that friend rings you? Or when you walk into a room do you instinctively know when there has been an argument as you can "cut the atmosphere with a knife?" or even just knowing what someone is thinking or what they are going to do? Well, I truly believe that we are tuning-in subconsciously and tapping in to our hidden psychic ability, which in effect is not really lost but buried deep within the subconscious.

However there are certain individuals in this world who claim never to have lost this amazing ability of psychic power and throughout their lives claim to have contact with discarnate souls or spirits of the deceased. We call these people psychic mediums and the genuine ones really are in the minority. They have somehow kept and developed this amazing ability. However a lot of people put situations like those aforementioned down to coincidences, but psychics do not believe in coincidences. Neither does the author for I have had over the years many experiences I would deem as psychic; however I do not regard myself as one of those gifted people who has hung on to and developed the power.

These experiences and more have led me to delve into the fascinating world of ghost-hunting, psychic power, and the paranormal. I believe that these subconscious psychic tune-ins are responsible for so many of us having paranormal experiences such as seeing ghosts and witnessing paranormal activity.

As far back as I can remember I have always had an interest in the paranormal. As a child I was fascinated with the idea of ghosts and things that go bump in the night, although the idea frightened me witless it never deterred me from taking an interest. Strange as it may seem, in a way the fear generated from paranormal activity (ghosts) gave me an adrenalin rush like nothing before. I used to enjoy being petrified out my wits and I still do to this very day.

When I was young I would ask my father to tell me ghost stories when I went to bed. He used to tell me one tale in particular about a little boy who used to live in our house many years ago, who one day was killed on the electric railway line at the back of the house. He was electrocuted. He would tell me that my bedroom was also the little boy's bedroom and on many occasions he would hear his footsteps cross the floor from downstairs as we were lying in bed fast asleep. He knew this because when he yelled up the stairs telling us to get back in bed, there was no reply, and on coming up the stairs to check this he would find the house in silence and my brother and myself were sure enough, asleep in our rooms. This story, kept me firmly in my bed absolutely terrified, and as it turned out it was a true story as I found out in later years when I questioned my father about it.

Introduction

The ghostly experiences I have had due to occasionally "tuning in" subconsciously you will read about in a later chapter. These episodes have led me into an adulthood of paranormal research and ghost-hunting and I know in my heart and mind that there are real ghosts and spirits out there on another level of existence. In this volume you will find detailed accounts of my paranormal investigations and ghost-hunts, which I have undertaken to try and prove this is so. There is also a section on light anomalies, or orbs, as they are commonly known, and I will try to answer the question that so many of us have asked, and that is; what is a ghost? I will then go into some detail on what equipment ghost-hunters use to try and track down the tormented and earthbound souls. I hope that you the reader will enjoy this journal of investigations and the history of my interest in this fascinating subject as much as I have enjoyed the investigations, the writing and the compiling of all the data herein.

The accounts you will read have been told exactly how they unfolded and no attempt has been made to glorify or exaggerate them in any way shape or form, this I promise. I am merely presenting the evidence I have collated from the paranormal investigations, and some findings I have made through my ghost hunts. In my opinion, ghosts are real and I have experienced them firsthand. How about you?

Chapter One

What is a Ghost?

A very interesting question indeed, and one which has been asked for many years - almost since the beginning of man and by all races and cultures across the globe. In all honesty and in my opinion, definite answers have still not been found and are being sought to this day. A ghost is described in the Collins English Dictionary as *a spirit, a dead person appearing again*; a sound and accurate description which I personally always thought a ghost was, and in my mind still is, but in modern times the term "ghost" is now defined in the eyes of the ghost hunter as a whole range of mysterious and inexplicable phenomena.

Ghosts these days are not just white figures walking through walls or phantoms of long-dead humans beings seen long after their deaths, but a huge array of alleged phenomena ranging from smells to sounds and feelings. For example smells such as tobacco and lavender are often deemed as ghostly when the smell has no apparent reason for being there; the smell of flowers, especially roses, is common as is pipe smoke too.

Auditory phenomena are quite common with noises like taps and raps, breaths and sighs, the rustling of dresses and many more that could be mentioned and interpreted as being ghosts. Visual phenomena are also very common with things such as ghostly fog or mist being seen. Black shadows moving around in dark and foreboded places, and the most common visual phenomenon these days to rear its head is the light anomaly; luminous strips and glowing spheres alleged to be spiritual energy, picked up mostly on cameras but every now-and-again seen with the naked eye. (See my theory on these remarkable light anomalies later in this volume). It is also believed that an oppressive feeling along with a cold atmosphere in what would normally be a warm and welcoming environment is deemed as being a ghost, along with impressions people pick up on that make them feel ill-at-ease, again in what would normally be a friendly atmosphere.

But are all these examples really actual ghosts? Would it not be fairer to say that this and all the alleged phenomena aforementioned could actually be the manifestation of a ghost and what it can produce, and not the ghost itself? This brings me back to my original thought. I always believed that a ghost was the image of a dead person, spirit or soul of a deceased individual that was seen after that person's loss of physical life. This now brings me to ask a number of questions: How does a ghost or spirit of a person come to be? Why do we see them? How do we see them, and what are their purposes?

One common theory is that of the "stone tape", place-memory or psychic recording ghost when past actions and scenarios that have previously been played out in life (normally the violent and traumatic ones) can somehow be recorded by the fabric of the buildings or surrounding areas in which they occurred, and every once in a while they are played back to those people who tune in to their psychic powers and receive these images from the past. Very interesting concepts indeed, but with all these ideas and theories nothing to my knowledge has ever been proved.

Another common explanation is that ghosts are the souls of the dead. Some believe that we in our physical bodies are spirits in the incarnate, that is to say the physical body we are given is the capsule or shell for the soul or spirit to live in during the physical life.

When the body dies the soul or spirit is thought to move on as a discarnate soul - the spirit or soul without the body. Where? That is another debate in itself but some believe that the good souls go to heaven and the bad ones go to hell, others believe that they are reborn again in a new physical form, hence the term re-incarnation. However the souls that get lost in the afterlife are the ones thought to be ghosts. So why do these lost souls haunt the living? A popular belief is that we are haunted for a reason, unlike the psychic recording or stone-tape residual ghost, some are said to be able to interact with us in order to right a wrong or fulfil a task that was not done in life.

In Charles Dickens's *A Christmas Carol*, this type of haunting is depicted by a number of ghosts visiting Ebenezer Scrooge in the night to try and help him see the errors of his ways. Once the task has been done, the ghost appears no more. Although a classical ghost story, accounts just like this are reported the world over. Some ghosts are said to foretell a death when an apparition is seen, and some are believed to bring good news or warn people of impending danger. However a lot of ghosts are said to be just the aimless wonderings of lost souls with no purpose and no meaning at all. Crisis apparitions or ghosts of the living are fascinating too. They, as well as spirits of the departed are an incredible concept in which many of these cases have been documented. These involve a phantom or an image of a person who is actually still alive at the time of the appearance. These apparitions are said to be a harbinger of death.

A well-documented case of this type of ghost is that of a certain admiral in the navy who was at sea with his fleet of ships. Many miles away in London the apparition of the admiral appeared to his wife who was at their family home. Unbeknown to her at the time, the admiral's ship was sinking and ultimately his fate was sealed. A very interesting kind of ghost to say the least. These ghosts I have discussed can be somewhat frightening and nerve-racking should you suddenly come across one, but it has to be said that never has a ghost like the ones aforementioned caused anyone any physical harm or hurt in any way. However there is an exception to the rule as they have occasionally been documented to assault and lash out at people. It has to be the most frightening paranormal experience anyone could have, and that is of the poltergeist. The word poltergeist derives from two German words; *polter* means to knock or rap or generally be noisy, and *geist*, meaning ghost. - noisy ghost.

And noisy is an understatement. If you have ever experienced poltergeist activity there is no doubt that it leaves you shaken up and very frightened indeed, as it did with the author in Dieppe in France in 1986. Although it was an isolated incident it will stay with me for the rest of my life and it is something I will never forget. Before I explain a few theories about what the poltergeist is believed to be, first let me tell you about my encounter with a one.

At the age of thirteen I was taken to Dieppe with the school for a week and I stayed in a huge, old mansion, which had been converted into a centre for schools. It lay off a winding, old country road and was hidden deep behind a copse of trees. It had rooms converted into dormitories with a very religious feel to the whole place, as crucifixes were on nearly all the walls and portraits of

Christ were in abundance. There were approximately six dormitories. The biggest slept about 25, and the smallest slept about 5–6. I was in one of the small ones with one of my school friends and four pupils from another school.

It all started during the last day when we smuggled some fresh orange juice up the stairs and into the dorm. We were not allowed to take food or drink into the bedrooms, and I spilled nearly half the carton onto the wooden floor. Instead of washing it up correctly I had one of my dorm colleagues help me lift up my bedside cabinet (which took the two of us to carry), and placed it over the stain we had left in the middle of the floor, not thinking that if the teacher had came in to the dormitory the first thing he would have asked would have been, "Why is your bedside cabinet in the middle of the floor?" Anyway it stayed there for the rest of the day. Night time came and we went to our beds. It wasn't long before we were all out for the count, and throughout the night I was woken by the sound of a slow, continuous knocking. I opened my eyes and thought to myself, "What on earth is that?" as it was coming from within the room itself.

As I turned and looked into the darkness of the room I could see the bedside cabinet that we had moved earlier in the middle of the floor, slowly rocking from side to side, I watched this for about twenty seconds. It was balancing on one side of the bottom, coming to rest, as it should stand normally, creating the knocking sound as it came to rest on the floor, and then tilting up the other way on to the other side of the bottom. No one was next to it yet it kept on rocking and balancing perfectly. I couldn't believe what I was seeing so I slid my legs off the side of the bed (the bottom bunk) and put my feet on the floor.

The cabinet still rocking, I wiped my eyes in utter disbelief, and then lunged forward to take a closer look, and what happened next I would never forget for the rest of my life. As I leant forward the cabinet in the middle of the room violently threw itself across the dormitory throwing my belongings everywhere from within and creating a crash that nearly burst my eardrums. Needles to say I ran for the light switch, crying in absolute terror, whilst the rest of my dormitory colleagues woke up with a fright saying, "What on earth was that?" I was hysterical and my friends were shocked too, to find the cabinet almost wrecked and my belongings all over the place. We left the light on for the rest of the night and needless to say we did not get any more sleep. We sat up together and chatted until breakfast. We packed our suitcases and thankfully left, as it was the last night in France and it was just as well as I couldn't have stayed another night in that room. So what was it that so abruptly woke us from our sleep that night? As with the other ghosts and hauntings there are no definite answers, only speculations.

One of the theories to explain these poltergeist phenomena is that it is exactly what the German term describes it as, and that is a *noisy ghost*; A malevolent and evil spirit hell-bent on causing disruption and mayhem for whoever or whatever it may be centred on - whether it be a place - centred haunting or a human focus, but nine times out of ten it is focused on a human, (almost in every case a female child or a young teenager.

However, a more common theory which is much more accepted these days is that the poltergeist is not a ghost or demon at all, but the telekinetic (TK) or psychokinetic (PK) mind of a disturbed and adolescent child. Telekinesis and psychokinesis are powers, which cause objects to be moved with the mind, or manipulate inanimate objects without physically touching them. However we have to look at what is termed as recurrent spontaneous psychokinesis (RSPK) and this is when the objects are moved and thrown about when the person responsible *is not aware* of their actions. The theory goes that when a youngster is growing up and is traumatised in some way (or is abused either mentally or physically at home or outside the home, perhaps being bullied at school, or their parents are being divorced etc), that certain individuals bottle up their emotions and anger, and it will not be long before something has to blow, so to speak.

Normally it would be in the form of a temper tantrum and it is dealt with there and then. However in extreme cases these individuals, or poltergeist *focii*, cannot release their emotions and anger and so a psychic energy is created and built up within the individual. When that person reaches puberty for some reason this energy is released in the form of recurrent spontaneous psychokinesis (RSPK); a subconscious, psychic temper tantrum if you will. This person releasing the psychic energy is unaware of his or her actions as it is being done with the subconscious mind so the outcome for that individual and the people close to them is somewhat terrifying. To see things being violently thrown around without anyone there to do it is a harrowing experience. This theory is an absolutely fascinating one and, if it was proven to be valid, and the cause of a poltergeist is not really a ghost or spirit, it still leaves us with fantastic evidence of psychic power and the ability to do fantastic things with the subconscious mind. Either way, the phenomena would be proved. So does this chapter answer the question, "What is a ghost?"

What you have just read are merely the opinions of many, many people. I have learned about these opinions and ideas over my years of research and I have also, of course, formed my own thoughts and opinions and came to my own conclusions through the experiences I have had. I will leave you with one final thought. Seeing is believing, and if you see a ghost, or if you see furniture fly across the room of its own volition as I have, you will know! And you will believe! However, trying to convince someone of this you will never accomplish, and they may never believe unless that person sees for himself or herself. So it all boils down to personal experience and forming your own opinions. I know what mine are.

Chapter Two

My Interest in the Paranormal.

My earliest recollection of paranormal activity was at about the age of ten. It was when I was sent to bed and I was the only one in the house upstairs. Since my brother was three years older than myself he was allowed to stay up a little longer than me, which really annoyed me because deep down I knew I did not want to be upstairs on my own. As I lay in bed trying to get to sleep with the landing light left on, I often heard the sound of the stairs creaking as if some one was creeping up them. Now most people would say that old houses creak anyway. However, the difference here is that it seemed that every creak or noise the stair made coincided with what noise would have been made if somebody were actually ascending the staircase. Some stairs made some recognisable and distinguishing noises and some stairs did not make any noise at all.

I became convinced that someone was creeping up the stairs. As I lay there frozen in my bed, the noises on the stairs become louder as though whoever or whatever was making its accent was getting closer to my room. The noises on the stairs kept on coming as I became more frozen with fear until they reached the top of the stairs. I thought it may have been my mother or father checking up on me to make sure I was asleep, but on calling out I had no response, which scared me even more. I soon began to realise that whoever or whatever was present was now standing behind my bedroom door and it always seemed to stop there, every time this happened. Then as I was lying there in total silence I could here the distinctive noise of slow breathing emanating from behind the door. At this point I screamed for my parents as I was petrified. I heard the downstairs door open and can remember hearing the voices of my father, mother and brother at the bottom of the stairs and in the living room, which clearly indicates to me that it could not have been a family member creeping about. This happened on countless occasions and I am convinced I heard what I heard.

I was wide-awake and I was positive I was not imagining any of it. I can still remember this like it was yesterday as I can with all of my other encounters with the paranormal, which I will elaborate upon now. Thinking back on this whole episode I am still convinced to this day that something strange was happening on the stairwell in my old house.

Footsteps on the Old Railway Line

Another encounter I had as a youngster occurred on a stretch of railway line at the back of the old house. I was playing with my friends in the grounds of the old Hawthorn Leslie factory (now St Peters basin) when I realised it was time to go home. I said goodbye to them and told them I would see them later. I started to climb up the steep embankment and up to the railway line next to the scrap yard.

As I was walking home along the railway I suddenly became aware of someone behind me following me along. I knew this as I heard their footsteps right behind me crunching along on the gravel. I turned around to see who it was and there was no one there. Now I knew the footsteps were directly behind me and no one could have hid in the time it took me to turn around. I stopped, had a quick look around and resumed my short journey home. Almost as soon as I started to walk again I heard the footsteps, only this time they sounded even closer. I turned around again - this time starting to panic a little - and still there was no one there. I then ran home as fast as I could.

The Breeze from Beyond?

A short but nevertheless interesting incident occurred one night as a teenager when I was asleep in my bed and all of a sudden I was awakened by a constant flow of wind blowing against my forehead. I could feel the cold as it hit me and when I put my hands up and wiped my head the breeze kept coming. It felt as if there was an invisible "someone" in the room blowing on my forehead (as if blowing on a hot cup of tea to cool it down).

After twenty seconds or so it stopped. Now at the time my bed was in the corner of the room and was nowhere near the window, which was closed anyway, and I was facing the wall. I had completely awoken by then and was mystified as to what it was; the room normally had no draughts, not like the one I felt that night and it is still a mystery today as it was then.

The Dead Boy?

It was a hot night and it was time to go to bed. After I had lain down I slowly started to heat up so I took off my t-shirt and went to sleep. It was during the night I woke up and for some reason I felt really unnerved, I then noticed standing in my doorway the shadow or silhouette of a young boy roughly about ten years old. All I wanted to do was reach across for the t-shirt, which was on the floor, and put it on, (never mind the fact there was what appeared to be the ghost of a young boy at the door of my room). This I did and for about two minutes I lay in my bed and stared at this small silhouette of a boy. The next thing I remember was waking up in the morning. I must have fallen back to sleep, and my first thoughts were, "What a strange dream I had" until I got out of bed and I realised that my t-shirt was back on - only back-to-front and inside -out. So I *did* get up in the night and put on my t-shirt! Which raises the question, why? Was the boy really in my doorway after all? I can't say for sure, it may have been the ghost of the young boy who once lived in my old house, or it may have been a dream. I cannot say it was a ghost, and I can't say it wasn't.

Nevertheless it was quite disturbing, thinking how vivid the whole episode was and the fact that I felt the apparition was looking at me and could very well have been thinking, "Who are you and what are you doing in my bedroom?" But it was the poltergeist experience in France (mentioned in Chapter One) that convinced me something strange was definitely going on out there in the world of the paranormal, and it also made me think about the other experiences I had as a youngster. They too, in my mind, were more real now than they ever were, and I was convinced ghosts and psychic disturbances were very real indeed. The French episode frightened me and confused me immensely yet I still craved to learn more.

These were just some of my experiences I had as a youngster, so you can now imagine and begin to understand why I had this strange obsession with fear and the will to understand it, and also the interest I have in this fascinating subject. I always wanted to experience and learn more about supernatural / paranormal phenomena, so I read books about ghosts, UFOs, psychic powers, telepathy, ESP and spirituality, which I then kept to form a fantastic library which I have to this day.

Becoming a Ghost Hunter.

The years went by and the more I read and learned about the paranormal the more I wanted to research this fascinating subject and get involved with some real life ghost - hunting and case studies. It seemed the experiences I had, as a youngster were depleting as I was getting older and I suppose it was curiosity that drove me into full-on paranormal research.

I truly believe that as I grew older I lost my ability to tune in to these things (as I outlined in the introduction) and I wanted to experience them again. Ghost-hunts and research were the answer. I became involved with a number of research societies and ghost-hunting groups until I decided to form my own team. I called it *"The North East Ghost In-Spectres"*.

Chapter Three

A tribute to *Harry Price.* The Father of Modern Day Ghost Hunting.

In my opinion Harry Price was the greatest, most enthusiastic ghost hunter and psychic researcher that has ever lived. A self-proclaimed "professor of the paranormal" his investigations at Borley Rectory on the Essex and Suffolk border between 1929 and his untimely death in 1948 is what caught my attention as a youngster growing up. Techniques and methods used to catch ghosts in action and prove the authenticity of alleged hauntings were pioneered by Harry Price and are still used to this day by ghost hunters and paranormal investigators the world over.

Harry Price was also an amateur conjurer (his interest in magic began at the tender age of eight years) and an inventor, and the inventions he made were specifically built and used to test spiritualist mediums from all over the world. Nine times out of ten he proved them to be fraudulent. Harry Price himself at this point did not believe that a human being could produce paranormal phenomena in the way that these mediums claimed and put what they produced down to magic or trickery. Being a member of the Magic Circle and knowing how to create illusion it was not hard for Harry Price to expose these fraudulent charlatans.

His father was a travelling salesman for a firm of paper manufacturers and after trying his hand at several lines of work, which included manufacturing glue and photographing shop-fronts in London, Harry himself entered this line of work, becoming a salesman for the same company as his father.

It might come as a revelation to readers who have read about the great Harry Price in the past to know that in fact he never left this line of employment. Despite being well-known as a famous ghost-hunter Price never gave up his day job and worked in the paper industry all his life and his working class background was one of the factors that affected his relationship with his colleagues in the field of psychical research in which he became active after the 1st World War. In 1908 Harry Price married Constance Mary Knight and the couple set up home in the village of Pulborough in West Sussex where they would live for the rest of their lives. Constance had the benefit of a small trust fund that supplemented Price's income as a travelling salesman and enabled him to establish what would become - and still is to this day - the greatest library of literature on magic, conjuring and the occult in the world.

This magnificent collection is now housed at Senate House in London University along with the Harry price Library that consists of hundreds of books, documents, reports and photographs that he amassed over the years as a psychical researcher. His life's work was bequeathed to the university after his death and can be seen by appointment.

Harry Price's involvement with psychical research in Britain began when he was elected a member of the Society for Psychical Research (SPR) in June 1920. After six years he was not happy with the way the society was going, so on the 1st of January 1926, Harry Price founded the National Laboratory of Psychical Research and it opened in Queensbury Place, London with himself as the honorary director. This had involved nearly a year of not only hard work but also considerable personal expense on Price's part as he had equipped the facility to an impressive standard out of his own pocket. After the birth of his National Laboratory of Psychical Research Harry Price investigated dozens of cases both here and abroad. Some of the cases he documented were very strange indeed. But Harry Price was a clever man and was also a controversial person who loved his publicity. A number of these cases were well thought-out and well-executed publicity stunts, which brought worldwide attention to his laboratory and his work.

A great example of this was back in 1927 when a box was mysteriously left at his laboratory while he was out on business somewhere. The box was alleged to have belonged to an eighteenth century prophetess called *Joanna Southcott*. In 1814 she left this curious box with a friend after she died and gave strict instructions saying that the box must only be opened during a national crisis and also specified that there must be twenty-four bishops present when the box was opened. This box was very well known - as was Joanna Southcott in the early 1900s - and Harry knew this would bring big publicity. Unbeknown to the general public (and the media) Harry Price had the box X-rayed prior to the massive public opening where the media were in abundance and he knew fine well the box was actually full of odd and curious items and contained nothing at all of any interest. Ingenious.

Another one of Price's publicity stunts or unorthodox cases (no one knows for sure) was the haunting of Cashen's Gap in 1935. It is better known as "*The case of Gef, the Talking Mongoose*". In a lonely farmhouse in the remote area of Cashen's Gap on the Isle of Man, it was reputed that a haunting of the more, lets say, unorthodox kind was taking place. The farmhouse owners claimed they were being haunted by a disembodied voice that spoke to them on a number of occasions. They also claimed the voice was not that of a human, but that of a mongoose! Harry Price heard about the case and promptly visited the house with co-researcher R S Lambert to investigate. The two investigators subsequently published a book on their investigations and name it *The Haunting of Cashen's Gap.*

Another of Harry Price's controversial claims came during a séance at a house in London in 1937. During the séance he claims to have met the materialized spirit of a six-year-old girl called Rosalie. By all accounts Harry was alleged to be deeply troubled and shaken up by this whole experience and this was (according to Harry himself) one of the few cases that he was actually convinced by. Along with the examination of the Rudi Schneider case in 1929, these were what convinced him there was indeed truth in spiritualism and contacting the dead. Again, this controversial claim brought him massive media attention worldwide. A publicity stunt? Or was Harry telling the truth? I guess we will never know for sure.

It was in June 1929 when his biggest case came. During his investigations with Rudi Schneider he was contacted by the editor of the *Daily Mirror* and was informed about a haunted house in the Home Counties. He visited the tiny hamlet of Borley, which lay on the Essex and Suffolk borders, as apparently the old Victorian rectory built in 1863 was being plagued by horrendous poltergeist and ghostly activity. However he didn't get enthusiastic about the case until some time after his initial visit in June 1929. He visited Borley again in 1931, and thought that Marianne Foyster was playing tricks and was responsible for the alleged phenomena. He subsequently expressed this thought to her husband Lionel Foyster and they parted on bad terms. He didn't take the case seriously until he had read Lionel Foyster's diary of occurrences, which he compiled while living at Borley Rectory. Then, after seeing Edwin Whitehouse's written accounts of his experiences while at this huge Victorian red brick monstrosity, he was forced to reconsider and took the case on. This would be towards the mid 1930s.

This case turned out to be his most famous, it was also believed by some (including Harry) to be one of the best, and most authenticated cases of ghost and poltergeist activity in history and some people today think that this is still the case. It was this case he continued to work on and investigate, on and off, until his death in 1948.

He had already written two best-sellers on the hauntings and was preparing a third volume when he sadly died. The last nineteen years of his life were spent investigating Borley Rectory. Harry was unfortunately blamed by his critics for a lot of the phenomena that occurred at the rectory, and was accused of fraud. But what makes the haunting of Borley Rectory stand out more than any of the other cases was the fact that the phenomena had been reported for quite a while even before Harry Price's involvement. The amount of single, independent witness accounts since the building was constructed in 1863 until its demolition in 1944 was incredible, and ran into hundreds. Even after the demolition of the rectory in 1944 after it had burned down in 1939, reports still came in of ghostly goings-on at Borley and even after Harry Price's death the accounts still came in. The last sighting of the infamous Borley Nun came in the 1970s. So, whether or not Harry Price did indeed fabricate a little, (which, I have to say was never proved) it seems that Borley Rectory was indeed haunted and was one of his more serious and more authenticated cases.

To this day people still believe in the authenticity of the Borley case and this is what the great Harry Price is remembered for. Just before his death in 1948 he was liaising with a talented and up-coming ghost-hunter and researcher called Peter Underwood. Harry price was a member of the ghost club and asked Peter to join. He did, and subsequently became the president and still is to this day. Harry Price had arranged to meet Peter Underwood but Harry Price's death occurred just a few days before the arranged date. Since Harry Price's death, Peter Underwood took over from him in documenting and investigating the Borley Rectory case and has spoken to all living witnesses in relation to the Borley saga. He too favors Harry Price and agrees that Borley was indeed a genuine case. He wrote a book called *The Ghosts of Borley Rectory* with Price's biographer Paul Tabori, based on his findings. To date Peter Underwood FRSA, has written no less than forty-six books and is now the world's leading paranormal investigator and ghost-hunter. Whatever the sceptics and the cynics say about Harry Price, the memory and work of this remarkable man still live on through people like Peter Underwood, and in my personal opinion he will never be forgotten.

Chapter Four

The Orb and Light Anomaly Phenomenon.

Orbs; just what are they? That is the question I have been asking myself since these light anomalies came to the public's attention. Having said that, they have allegedly been around from the start according to the psychics, but only recently have these round, glowing balls of light - believed to be the first stage in a ghost materialisation - been caught on night vision video cameras and digital still cameras. Hereward Carrington said in his 1970s book, *Your Psychic Powers and How to Develop Them* that at the beginning of ghostly materialisations you would see light spots before your eyes. Could he mean orbs? These would be followed by a white mist and then the full materialisation of the spirit itself. This is just one of many theories put forward as to how a ghost comes to be seen.

Very occasionally these orbs have been caught on normal 35mm cameras and if you are really lucky they can be seen with the naked eye. Well, I decided to do some tests and research to find out if these so-called spiritual spots, or spirit light-energies, were real or not and if they were indeed linked to the world of ghosts and apparitions.

Are they merely dust particles, moisture or digital camera defects, as a lot of people seem to think, or are they really spiritual energy? It all started when modern-day ghost-hunters and the like were getting their photographs back after investigations and finding upon them round, anomalous balls of light. Some were larger than others and some were brighter than others; some of them were even different colours. You could see through some of them and some were milky white, but there was one thing they all had in common: They were only photographed and seen in places known to have spiritual activity; in other words they were only caught in haunted locations.

I first heard about the orb phenomenon when I heard people talking about their photos on a late-night radio phone-in show. I had been interested in ghosts and the paranormal for a long time and had never heard of these light anomalies before, so why all of a sudden were they now coming to light? I wanted to see if I could catch these elusive spheres of souls for myself so I decided to visit more haunted sites and take more photos. I also checked my collection of older photos that I had previously taken on other field trips and investigations and found nothing at all that resembled these orbs so I concentrated on taking new photos. As mentioned earlier, it is believed because of modern technology that these spots of light were easier to capture on digital cameras. So I purchased one - but not before I ventured up to a Castle in Northumberland with my little 35mm camera on 31 October (of all nights) when the castle was opened for Halloween.

On the evening in question we were looking around the castle when one of the party I was with said she had seen two of these orbs with her naked eye floating about at the top of one of the rooms. I never got a chance to see them, even though I was in the same room; nevertheless when it was brought to my attention that orbs had been seen, I asked whereabouts in the room they were. When I was told about this I pointed my 35mm camera in that direction and took one, single frame.

When I got my photographs back there were two or three perfectly round, glowing orbs right in the same place they were seen with the naked eye. Could these orbs be real, genuine spirit energy as they were seen with the naked eye and then caught on 35mm film? I don't think dust could light up the way this witness described them, at least not with the naked eye, anyway. As my witness said, they were just floating around near the top of the room and they were round and bright; then they were gone. These were my first orbs caught on camera and I was overjoyed, but I still wanted to know more. Since that night I have managed to catch a number of orbs with my 35mm, but not many. It was not until I acquired my Olympus c150 digital camera that I started to pick up many more of these orbs. Now I was coming back with orbs on my photographs but I still did not understand exactly what they were. I decided to conduct some test and experiments to see if I could reproduce these light anomalies.

The first of a number of experiments I carried out was to see if we could reproduce the orb effect with dust particles. The idea was born after I had been to a judo club in a community centre at Byker, which also has a reputation for being haunted, and had put down the mats on the floor and later took photos of the judo in progress. Lo and behold I caught what looked like orbs on my pictures and I thought it possible that it was because of all the dust we had kicked up whilst putting down the mats.

This is when I started to rethink and question for myself, the orb phenomenon. My first real test was when I ran an investigation in a castle near Alnwick. It was a small but simple test. During the investigation I sat down on one of the old settees in the apartment and out shot from down the side of the settee a puff of dust! At that point after waiting a few moments I pointed my camera in the area of where the dust shot out and took a couple of shots. They contained what looked to be orbs, indicating that specs of dust can and do produce orb-like anomalies.

To further this test and to be sure dust particles can explain a lot of the orb phenomenon I conducted another test during an investigation in a castle on Tyneside. Whilst a colleague of mine was filming with his infra-red night vision camera, we decided to put a digital camera on top of the video camera in the hope the infra-red beam would help me pick up something anomalous. When my flash went off it lit up the dust particles and it give the orb effect. We determined this when we looked back at the video recording in slow motion. You can clearly see the reflection of the dust particle evolve into the ring of light from nothing, and then disappear, clearly indicating that these orbs are nothing more than light reflections from dust particles. If you shake dusty curtains or kick up dust and then wait a minute or two, you are guaranteed to photograph orbs. Other tests I have carried out have also proved that moisture in the air can reproduce the orb effect, as too can light raindrops, breath, fog or mist.

I feel that these tests and experiments do not eliminate the orb phenomenon completely as there are a number of orbs on photographs and on film, which I feel are very impressive and are a little harder to explain. This brings me to the light anomaly, which is seen with the naked eye. These are a lot more interesting and rule out moisture and dust reflections from the camera flash. However naked eye orbs (some, but not all I hasten to add) could be tricks of the light, light reflections from vehicles or cars in the vicinity, torch lamps or flashlights. I have been in situations and on investigations where I have seen light anomalies with the naked eye. On one occasion no outside light was able to penetrate and all equipment that could have given off light was turned off.

These are probably the best light anomalies I have personally witnessed and in all honesty I cannot explain them. These anomalies were not of the round, usual type either -although I have seen those too - but long, luminous strips. One really strange anomaly was actually triangular and was also seen by a fellow investigator. I believe it is down to the witnesses themselves whether or not they can determine if these orbs are deemed credible, and it is the investigator's job to rule out any of the aforementioned natural explanations. In my opinion about 95% of the orb phenomenon can be explained as outlined above. However an explanation for the remaining 5% of orbs or light anomalies seems to be eluding myself and the rest of the ghost-hunting fraternity.

I now turn my attention to the orbs caught on night vision video cameras and orbs caught in movement. The fact is that when some of these anomalies are caught on video we can see them moving around with speed and trajectory that dust or moisture, in my opinion, could never reproduce. However the rationalists and good, honest paranormal researchers sometimes put explanations forward - such as moths and insects - after inspecting them a lot closer; which is commendable, as we don't really want to delude ourselves. But this cannot explain them all as, on occasions, when we do inspect them closer, we can clearly see a small, round ball of light aimlessly floating around and disappearing. So that covers most of the theories and explanations of what these elusive light anomalies are. Of course a lot more investigation and research is needed to fully understand what I would deem to be genuine orbs and light anomalies, but for the time being I suppose the reader will have to make up their own mind. But if the psychics are to be believed, and orbs really are the first stages in a ghost materialisation, it would be amazing to think, now in the 21st Century, that we are starting to photograph genuine spiritual energy - possibly ghosts.

Chapter Five

Ghost Hunting Equipment.

Contrary to what most people think, on paranormal investigations and ghost hunts a ghost will not appear before your eyes and walk straight through a wall unless you are very fortunate indeed. More often than not I return from an investigation and friends and colleagues will ask," Well, did you see a ghost then?" and the vast majority of the time I have to be brutally honest and say, "No, I have not". Ghosts and spirits are not like trained dogs, and in that respect I mean they do not appear on demand, and they certainly do not jump through hoops just because you are there to see them. So, what is the ghost hunter's job and why do we do it? Very good questions indeed in which I often find asking myself from time to time.

Ultimately we would all like to see the full-blown apparition or ghost, and even more we would like to capture its movements on video camera or 35mm camera film. Other than that, there are some tell-tale signs that denizens of the other world are not far away and it is these signs we try to record and document to at least gather some sort of viable evidence in the hope that, one day, we can prove the existence of ghosts. To trace and record these signs we use an array of gadgets and devices we call "ghost-hunting equipment". I personally believe that the best tools of the trade are our five senses; sight, sound, taste, smell and touch. But of course there are some individuals who claim to hold a sixth sense, and there are two of these people on the team to assist in our investigations. Along with team psychics we use other appliances and devices to help in our endless search for spectres of bygone days. I will now outline some tools of the trade and explain the hypothetical reasons why they are used.

Electro-Magnetic Field (EMF) Meters.

These devices are used normally for measuring the natural electro-magnetic field emissions within houses, offices, etc. It is known that TVs, clock radios, refrigerators and other electrical appliances such as computers emit what are known as EMFs. If one is subjected to these EMFs over a long period of time it can prove fatal as research shows they can, in extreme cases, cause cancer. The EMF-meter was designed to detect how much actual EMF pollution these appliances give off and gives advice on where to put these appliances in the home so as to create as little risk as possible from potential exposure.

It is believed by psychics and ghost hunters alike that when a ghost or spirit tries to move something (perhaps a bunch of keys or an item of furniture), or to materialise (show itself in its full ghostly form), it needs to draw energy from somewhere in order for this to be achieved. The electro-magnetic field is said to be the primary and most favourable choice and when this happens there is an alleged fluctuation or distortion within the natural electro-magnetic field.

On investigations we sometimes find perfectly good

working cameras and torches suddenly go dead on us and it literally leaves us in the dark. When we leave the location the torch or camera somehow restores its power and works fine once more. Nevertheless brand new batteries are required as there may have been a total power loss. It is thought a close-by entity may be responsible for this and is commonly known as "drainage". The EMF meter is used to detect any anomalies within this electro magnetic field.

Digital Thermometers and Temperature Reading Devices.

It is said that when a ghost or spectre is close-by the surrounding air and atmosphere tends to go ice-cold. This is called a temperature drop and these thermometers and temperature-reading devices are used in order to trace and record these temperature anomalies.

Night vision Video Cameras

Ghosts are said to be afraid of natural light but I do not believe this at all. Most ghost sightings tend to be when they are least expected and more often than not they are during the day. The theory goes that by using night vision video cameras / infra-red night vision cameras the device can pick up anomalies and see things the human eye cannot in these pitch-black vigil conditions. On our investigations they have proved quite invaluable and quite often we may record what is now known as an *electronic voice phenomenon*. (EVP).

Dictation Machines and EVP

A dictation machine is used in order to try and record voices from beyond or ghostly, auditory phenomena.

These are usually locked in a room where people have heard ghostly voices or experienced loud bumps, or knocks that cannot be explained by any natural means. As mentioned earlier with the video cameras these too can often pick up unexplained noises that are not normally heard at the time of recording. This modern-day device is now known as an EVP recorder. An EVP recorder is a digital dictation machine and both electronic and audiocassette machine are used on investigations.

Motion Sensors and Beam Barriers

Motion sensors and beam barriers are used to detect motion in a locked-off room or passage where a ghost is alleged to walk (or glide as the case may be). When beam barriers are placed down either side of a corridor or a stairwell an infra-red beam acts as a tripwire so to speak and if anyone or anything breaks the beam, an alarm is tripped thus indicating someone – or something - has walked past. Motion sensors do more-or-less the same thing only they cover more of the room and act like a room alarm. Like the beam barriers if anything breaks the beam within the room an alarm will sound indicating this. The reason they are locked off is simply because the investigators know for sure that nobody or anything of this world will be able to trip the beam. The same principle for sound recording can apply to the dictation machines, EVP and video-recording equipment too.

Digital and standard 35mm cameras

Both of these types of cameras are used on our investigations. Digital cameras are good in that you can view your photographs almost immediately and delete any unwanted photos from the memory card and save any decent photos one might acquire. The only downfall with digital photography is that the cameras are prone to pick up reflections of dust particles, which are often mistaken for orbs or light anomalies. With a normal 35mm camera the dust reflections are somewhat reduced to the point of nonexistence, and any good photographs acquired on an investigation will have a negative. What is on the photo should be on the negative. The negative can then be examined.

It is sad but true that, with the use of digital photography and modern photographic software on computers, it is all to easy to fix, manipulate or fake good ghostly photos, and experts have not got anything to examine in order to prove authenticity - like a negative which a 35mm camera would have. Although I do use a digital camera on investigations, I prefer to use my good old 35mm Nikon SLR in which you can use cable release or time exposure for taking shots in the dark without the use of a flash which essentially rules out light reflections should one acquire any light anomalies or orbs.

Notepad, Pen, and a Watch

These are probably the most important of an investigator's tools simply because we need to take a detailed and accurate account of any anomalies recorded and events witnessed throughout the duration of the investigation. In order to compile a thorough investigation report this is of the utmost importance. To note down the times of occurrences and events as and when they occur is much preferable to jotting down notes after the investigation at the risk of forgetting important details and even subconscious elaboration of the incidents in question.

Darren W. Ritson

The Trigger Object

Invented by the pioneer of modern ghost hunting, Harry Price, the trigger object was used in the case of Borley Rectory in Essex, England between 1929 - 1939 and other cases he documented. Objects would move around on their own and often be thrown violently across the rooms. So objects such as ornaments on the mantelpiece and window-sills would be chalked around and left locked off in an empty room. If the ghosts and spirits moved any of these objects they would obviously be moved from the chalked lines thus indicating paranormal activity. The use of this simple but effective technique is still used to this day, as mischievous ghosts still like to move things around.

We often use this method with good results. It is normal procedure to train a video camera on the trigger object so should it be moved it would be caught on film. Trigger objects vary these days from coins to keys and even rubber ducks. Certain types of ghosts may interact with a certain type of trigger object, for example a spirit of a small boy may want to play with a trigger object of a toy car, or a ghostly smuggler or contraband thief may interact with old coins or jewellery. The trigger objects vary from investigation to investigation. In a poltergeist case, anything can be used, even furniture.

Dowsing rods and crystal pendulums

It is believed by some that spirit contact can be made by using dowsing rods and crystal pendulums. The theory goes that a spirit can use its energies to manipulate the crystal or rods in certain directions in order to answer questions put to it by the dowser. This technique I feel is controversial as subconscious movements of the dowser may be responsible for the movement of the rods or the crystal. However, in some cases unorthodox movement of the crystal cannot so easily be explained away, for example the crystal may move violently in a triangular motion, and sometimes it has been pulled out of the dowsers hand. Dowsing has been proven to work with water, and minerals so why can't it be used to dowse for spirit? For this reason we use them on the team.

The Séance

The séance is not so much equipment but a technique used on some investigations as a means to communicate with the deceased. Without going into too much detail, a circle is formed by the holding of hands either while standing up or seated around a table. A designated investigator, usually a spirit medium or a psychic, will lead the proceedings. However it has been known for a non-mediumistic person to lead the séance but this only happens on our investigations when a medium or psychic is present to supervise. Spirit contact would then be attempted by asking the spirits to acknowledge their presence in the forms of knocks, bumps, temperature changes, so on and so forth. It is also requested politely that they may attempt to show themselves to us.

Although I have felt, heard seen and sensed phenomena through controlled séances, I have yet to see a full apparition of a ghost as a result of psychic energy built up within the séance circle. Séances can be very physically and emotionally demanding for the sitters so care must be taken at all times. *I must now stress that séances are very dangerous indeed, physically and mentally, if they are not undertaken in the correct manner, or under the correct supervision of a medium or psychic. I would recommend if you are interested in this form of spirit communication you should visit your local spiritualist church and under no circumstances try them out for yourself.*

The Baseline Test

Prior to any of these techniques being applied on an investigation, a baseline test must be carried out on the venue, which is to be investigated. These tests will include temperature readings, along with EMF sweeps, so to determine the normal baseline readings of the rooms and locations.

Should any anomalies be traced and picked up on the investigation itself, we will have a detailed account and record of these readings to compare with so we can determine what is normal and what is paranormal. During a baseline test we also seek out creaky floorboards, draughty rooms and corridors, faulty doors, which may close on their own and other common, natural occurrences that are often mistaken for paranormal activity.

Chapter Six

The Community Spirit. Byker Community Centre Newcastle.

Byker Community centre is large three storey building situated in the East end of Newcastle and was built in 1928. Unlike the normal, new modern-day community centres this one has an unusual difference and boasts historical background. Inside the building there is a ground-floor basement and an apartment flat where the caretaker once would have lived. It has a spacious hall along with kitchens, an office on the ground floor and a huge, old ballroom and stage on the second floor.

Over the years the building has been used for an array of different things such as a church hall (it once belonged to the local church which stands adjacent to the community centre, and to this day stands on what is hallowed ground). The Boys Brigade and Girl Guides once frequented the building in years gone by, and as far back as records can show the building has always been used as a ballroom and dancehall for the more mature or elderly members of the community.

In more recent times activities such as badminton, table tennis and martial arts were often practiced in the building and since the early the 1990's there has been a Judo club there of which the author is a black belt and a former Judo instructor.

In the early days, before the centre was built, the land was the original Byker Farm and estate and in the 1920s the farm was demolished to make way for the community building. This magnificent grade-listed building survived the bombing raids of World War II and was used as a refuge and a hospital for the local victims of the bombing who lost their homes and were seriously injured or killed during 1939 - 1945. It goes without saying that some of these unfortunate victims of the German bombings would have died of horrific injuries inside this building. It is not hard to imagine the pain suffered by these unfortunate individuals; the hurting, the anguish and the torment of knowing nothing could be done to save them, all this may still somehow be recorded into the fabric of the building.

Being a member of the Judo club I was often in the building and I spent quite a bit of time chatting to the Community Workers who run and look after the place. They would often tell me stories about strange goings-on and how they thought ghosts inhabited the centre. I was told that on a number of occasions when the staff members were downstairs they often felt they were not alone and were being watched. When they turned around no one was there. Footsteps have also been heard in empty rooms but one of the more eerie stories was when the cleaner had came to work one morning and opened up the building and had reported that the piano on the top floor was playing. Upon a brave inspection the music stopped. She was the only person in the centre. A more sinister ghost is said to be seen gliding from one room to another on the ground floor and takes the form of a tall, black shadow. The former caretaker and odd job man told me he seen this spectre on a number of occasions. So we have a large, old building with a ghost on each floor. I also experienced the odd strange happening while in the centre on my own and, although I took great interest, I was not actually investigating the paranormal at that point in my life. However, in May 2003 I started my investigations and where better place to begin than the community centre at Byker. I knew the people there and I was a member.

I got permission to spend the night there and thus began a series of paranormal investigations into the alleged haunting of Byker Community centre. The first overnight investigation proved quite interesting to say the least as we recorded some interesting drops in temperature and more interestingly I actually heard the shuffling of feet and footsteps coming from the basement hall. Upon investigating I found the room empty. This, I thought, was a good time to leave my tape recorder locked off recording in there in the hope we picked up or recorded some paranormal activity. We were not disappointed because when I listened to the recording after the investigation I heard what I believed and still believe to be three or four distinct footfalls across the wooden floor, I had captured phantom footsteps and I knew this room was empty. All this combined with the *interior* doors at the entrance to the building violently rattling and shaking at about 3am proved our efforts were certainly not in vain.

Our team carried out a second investigation about one year later and this too proved interesting. We had the usual array of monitored activity such as the temperature drops, and photographic evidence of light anomalies etc, but the most interesting and frightening happening was when I was physically touched or grabbed on the arm in one of the storerooms off the basement hall. I nearly fell over trying to flee the room in terror, as I knew that no members of the team was next to me.

We left this room for a while and upon our return we could all feel a sense of foreboding coming from that room. It was also noted that when approaching the doorway to the room, the air was ice cold and it was like walking into a freezer, yet five minutes earlier the room was a nice ambient temperature. You could now see your breath it was that cold. There was something otherworldly in that room but who - or what - was it? We had a very sceptical and scientific-minded investigator with us that night and he was not sceptical for long. After an incident earlier on involving a door that slammed closed twice after we had secured it open, he was convinced something strange was definitely going on. This investigation proved too much for us and we closed it down at 3am and left the building.

We went back a month or two later to continue our investigations. The team arrived at 9.30pm and by 11.00pm we had started the investigation. What impressed me most about this investigation was that the new psychics we had asked along as guests picked up on events and happenings I know for a fact they could not have known about previously. This building cannot be researched on the Internet, coupled with the fact no one had even heard of the place prior to this investigation. All my results and findings from the previous investigations were kept under lock and key and nobody was aware of those results; neither did they know the ghost stories attached to the building.

Some absolutely amazing facts were produced by the psychics, including our team psychic Suzanne McKay, picking up on the fact that footsteps had been heard in the basement and the door upstairs was known to have slammed shut. Previous investigations proved this to be the case. Suzanne also picked up on - and told me exactly where - the ghost of a dark figure had been seen moving around on the ground floor. This was in the same spot where the former caretaker had seen the tall, black shadow glide from room to room. It was also picked up by our other team psychic, Glenn Hall, that the centre was used for a hospital or somewhere to tend to the wounded as he said he could sense surgical spirits and got the impressions of injuries and pain.

This is also correct as I take you back to the beginning of this chapter and remind the reader of the bombing in WWII and the injuries sustained by the very people taking refuge in the centre. One more piece of very impressive psychic ability was produced by one of the guest psychics. She told me while walking around the building that one or two people had passed on quite recently into the spirit world whilst in the building. She told me where she thought these people had died and how they died. It turns out she was correct with her impressions.

During this investigation while in the large hall on the second floor a guest investigator and developing psychic sat down next to where I know someone had passed on and claimed to see and feel someone sitting on the seat next to her. She got a bit of a fright when she realised it was not any of the team investigators. However for obvious reasons, and due to our code of ethics, I cannot name these people or state how they died. Needless to say these residual energies are still lingering in the community centre and are there to be picked up on by certain types of people at certain times. It must be stressed that these energies are just that; energy. These recently departed souls who passed into the spirit world are very likely resting in peace and the energy that is left over from years of visiting this centre is what is recorded into the building and this is what is left for the psychics to pick up on.

However I do feel that there are some active spirits and ghosts that do inhabit this old building and are quite mischievous to say the least. This conclusion has been deduced due to the fact that lots of strange, inexplicable occurrences have happened and have been recorded by *The North East Ghost In-Spectres*. There are also the tales and stories relayed to me by mature, credible and responsible witnesses. Although the building has not been around for a long time it's been around long enough to store, to record and house residual energies and active spirits, which essentially will still be there in years to come.

Chapter Seven

Wall-to-Wall activity The Schooner Hotel, Alnmouth

The Schooner Hotel is located on the Northumbrian coastline just a few miles south-east of Alnwick. Formerly a coaching in this 32 - bedroom hotel is claimed to be the most haunted hotel in Britain. No one knows exactly when this now - listed building was built, but it is said to be from around the 17th Century. The village of Alnmouth itself has a controversial and historical past as the Germans once bombed it during the Second World War. On 8th November 1941 two bombs hit the village; one in Argyle Street, and the other in a street not far away resulting in the deaths of many civilian people. Three houses were completely demolished.

On 6th September 1940, a spitfire from the 610 squadron based at Acklington crashed on the beach in Alnmouth. Flying officer C. H. Bacon was killed instantly. Going back even further, in the 13th century Alnmouth was hit by the plague and thus described by the Methodist John

Wesley, (who incidentally resided in the Schooner), as a place of all kinds of wickedness. The hotel too has a macabre past with stories of mass murders, suicides, smugglers and all kinds of mysteries during its 400-year history. The Schooner has also had its fair share of famous faces staying there, such as Charles Dickens who was of course famous for his ghostly novels. *A Christmas Carol* is one of my favourites, Basil Rathbone, Douglass Bader, and even King George III have made their stay there as well as the previously-mentioned John Wesley.

In more modern days the Schooner has become more famous for its ghostly inhabitants and paranormal activity, bringing ghost hunters from around the country to investigate. Tonight it was *The North East Ghost In-Spectres* turn to seek out the spooks and investigate this fantastic old haunted building.

On the night in question we arrived at The Schooner Hotel at 7.30pm and were met by the owners and current manager. We were informed of some of the strange goings-on and reports of recent paranormal activity that had been witnessed. Objects had been moving around on their own, doors had been seen and heard slamming shut and opening of their own volition, and, more eerily, a little girl has been seen running into one of the rooms. Upon inspection she was nowhere to be seen. These are just a few of the many hundreds of accounts and strange goings-on that have been reported over the last few years by the staff and visitors alike, making the hotel live up to its title *"The most haunted hotel in Britain, 1998 and 2002"*. Knowing this made it clear to the team where we should focus our investigation and what type of things to look out for. After scrutinising the establishment for draughts, creaky floorboards and other natural occurrences people often mistake for paranormal phenomena we were ready to begin the investigation.

We established our base room in which to leave our equipment and to take our breaks, and formed the plan of the investigation. For the first part of the "ghost hunt" we decided to stay together as a unit as the manager wanted to see the team at work as a whole. Armed with night vision video cameras, electro-magnetic field (EMF) meters which measure any anomalies within the natural electro-magnetic field, laser and digital thermometers to measure any anomalies in the temperatures, 35mm and digital cameras, and of course our team psychic, we headed of into the warren of corridors and rooms within the Schooner Hotel. From past investigations we knew the ghosts in the Schooner liked to play around with things and move/hide things such as peoples' belongings, keys etc, so we decided to draw around a number of bits and pieces and leave them locked off in some of the rooms in the hope that these spirits would interact with them and thus move them from their positions. If they moved we could tell by the lines we had drawn (a technique first used by Harry Price in the late 1800s and early 1900s).

This experiment is called "trigger object" and the reputation of the playful spirits of the Schooner proved fruitful to say the least as during the investigation, three of our locked off trigger objects were moved from their positions. Our base room was left unlocked when we went off to investigate, as we were the only personages in the hotel. When we returned for a break we found the door to be closed and locked. This happened twice during the course of the investigation and upon checking the lock we found nothing untoward; it worked fine, eliminating any faults the door may have had. We all left together and came back together so this rules out malicious trickery and deceit by anyone present, so who locked the door? It's a question that may never be answered. Among other phenomena recorded during the investigation were light anomalies or orbs caught in abundance on video and digital still camera, cold spots located and reported in various points in the hotel and sudden temperature drops noted and felt by all present. One temperature drop was a staggering eight degrees in three seconds flat in an area reputedly haunted by a psychotic killer who massacred his entire family hundreds of years ago. Although no actual ghosts were seen, I feel they were nevertheless ready to acknowledge their presence to us; of that I am convinced 110%.

On another investigation in early March 2005 – along with Team Phenomena - I was fortunate enough (or unfortunate as the case may be), to encounter one of the Schooner's many ghosts down by the kitchens in the corridor. Although I did not actually see anything I sure as heck heard strange and distinct footsteps coming from the darkness towards me. At the same time I felt a foreboding, threatening presence - and it was close by. Although I had ventured down there by myself I knew I was not alone. As I started to make my retreat I again heard these footfalls coming up the stairs behind me and they were even closer than before. It was at this point I ran like the wind along the dark corridor. I had only been down there for five minutes and that was enough. Running from ghosts and spooks is really the wrong thing to do, as after all, that was why we were there, but I suppose my natural survival instinct took over and I needed to just get out. My all too hasty escape resulted in my left wrist being almost broken and gashed open. I stubbed my toes and smashed my clipboard in half as I ran straight into a wall. In retrospect it is rather funny, but at the time I was absolutely terrified to say the least.

Tony Liddell, founder of *Otherworld North East*, who was also in attendance, administered first aid and checked me over and, only when he knew I was indeed alright, he marched me straight back down the corridor to where I had the encounter to make me literally face my fear. He believed that if I had not done this I may have not returned to ghost hunting and investigating; something he has seen before on other investigations. I believe he was right and for this I thank him. The investigation ended at 7.30 am and we decided to get some well-deserved sleep. We had a choice of any of the wonderfully haunted rooms so perhaps we would experience something else other-worldly while in our beds.

As it turned out we acquired some good quality, undisturbed rest and, after the night we had, we really needed it. Perhaps the ghosts and spectres of the Schooner Hotel had decided to let us rest in peace. After 400 years of history and haunting, perhaps it's about time they did too.

Chapter Eight

Train of Thoughts.
The Bowes Railway
and National Heritage
Museum, Springwell.

The Bowes National Heritage Railway Museum is situated in Springwell Village on the outskirts of Sunderland. The railway was opened in 1826 and was originally designed by the pioneer and creator of the modern steam engine, George Stephenson. The railway was built primarily to service a new colliery, which was sunk in Springwell in 1821 by John Bowes - already one of the most powerful men in the north's coal industry. The Springwell colliery continued the production of coal until its closure in 1932. In 1934–35 a lot of work was carried out to enlarge the mineshaft as there were plans to re-open the colliery, but due to complications during the work the idea was abandoned. The railway was intended to be worked by a combination of steam and gravity powered inclines and there was also a section ran by Stephenson's steam locomotives and covered a vast majority of South Tyneside, Durham, Gateshead and Wearside, transporting coal from collieries such as Dipton, Burnopfield, Ravensworth Anne, Ravensworth Shop, Heworth, and Wardley collieries to name a few. The coal would then be taken along to the Jarrow staiths where it would be shipped overseas. In 1940 the Springwell colliery was sold to the Washington Coal Company, who in turn passed ownership to the National Coal Board (NCB) in 1947, until the final closure of the colliery in 1970.

The mineshaft and some of the appendages belonging to the establishment were later demolished, however some were saved and restored and when the former colliery site was turned into the rail museum the remaining buildings were incorporated into the new complex. In the mid 1990's the area where the mineshaft stood was grassed over and a concrete marker now stands to mark the spot. Over the years Springwell has become home to the vast majority of locomotives and trains salvaged and rescued from the last colliery railways, making the site today a historical and nostalgic step back in time. Visitors can see these locomotives and also see how the old coal industry would have worked back in those days.

Between 1821 – 1932, when the coal industry was in its prime, it is believed that children as young as eight years-old were made to work down the mine. Needless to say, health and safety left a lot to be desired back in those days and a lot of unnecessary accidents would have - and did – occur. These resulted in many deaths of children and adults alike. Explosions rocked the colliery back in 1833, 1837 and again in 1869, killing literally hundreds of mine workers and seriously injuring dozens more. In more recent years it is reported that other deaths and accidents have occurred and even one suicide has taken place here. So the history of Bowes Railway is both a sad and bloody one.

I wanted to find out more about the site and hence arrange a paranormal investigation. I spoke to the manager of the museum, who told me a few of the ghostly tales and odd happenings that have occurred in recent times. I asked him if he had witnessed anything out of the extraordinary. He vouched forth and told me that he and a colleague had heard footsteps crunching along the gravel outside one of the wagon shops, and had thought someone was on their way to see him. When he went out to greet whoever it was, he found no one to be there. On looking around for anyone no one could be seen. Another strange story concerns a mysterious figure being seen making his way through the engineering room and disappearing at the top. When staff tried to locate this stranger, once again no trace of him could be found.

In the joiners' room the owners' dogs will not under any circumstances venture up the stairs to the former hayloft, they seem to be scared of something up there, he told me. He also told me that he had once heard the sound of children's laughter and reported seeing strange lights when working on his own in one of the workshops when the site was closed to the public. So who was responsible for the laughter? The phantom footsteps outside the wagon shop? Who is the mysterious man seen walking up the engineering room and disappearing without a trace? And why will the dogs not venture into the former hayloft? These are some of the questions *The North East Ghost In-Spectres* hoped to try and answer on the investigation.

Joining us on the Investigation was API founding members Cindy Nunn and Jo Carnegie along with some other guest researchers. The site is rather large so I needed to assemble a first-rate group of investigators in order to cover the site properly and to make sure the investigation was accurately documented.

On the night in question we arrived on site and started the investigation at 11.00pm. We split into groups, making sure the psychics on hand were in different groups. The investigation started off quite well with Suzanne McKay picking up on a shift of spiritual energy. She also sensed the man that walks in the engineering room. She said his name was Edward Chapman, but he preferred the name Eddie. During this vigil she also picked up on a man who had suffered extreme pain in his head and got the feeling of "his head being trapped". Very interesting indeed, as the records show a man once had his head crushed in between two trains. During our vigil the only "non-psychic" as it were experienced an icy-cold blast of wind, which was noticeably colder than the surrounding air. It hit him on the arm and chest area. Upon taking a photograph in that same area we caught an odd-looking light anomaly.

Our second location was the Joiners' Room and former hayloft, and upon entering this location an eerie, cold feeling was noted by all group members. Suzanne then asked where the stables were, as she got the "impression" of horses. (Please bear in mind, the psychics new nothing about these locations prior to the investigation nor did they know this area was a former hayloft).

As it turned out there were stables on site that were located just outside this building, standing adjacent to Springwell Lane. They housed the horses and ponies that were once used for "working the yards". When the pit ceased operation, the block was surplus to requirements and therefore demolished. A presence was then felt on the stairwell and all were in agreement that the stairs did have a certain feel to them. It was noted that whoever resided on the stairwell was merely an observer, just watching what goes on. Movement was then seen on the stairs by an investigator when all other investigators are elsewhere in the room. Following this we all heard several loud bangs and distinct thumps emanating from within the room and the source of these knocks could not be traced. An investigator then starts to feel unwell and the room temperature dropped by 5 degrees; sure signs of paranormal activity. We then called out, trying to communicate with whatever was in the room with us. Another two loud knocks were heard. Suzanne picked up on the name "John Bowes", and, when she mentioned this, she felt a cold breeze across her face. Was John Bowes in the room with us? It was a very interesting vigil indeed.

Our next location for investigation was the Wagon Shop, formerly a massive open-top coalbunker used when the pit was in operation. We made ourselves comfortable and began our observations. Suzanne, once more, astounded us all by saying the trains in there were "not at home", and "shouldn't be here". She then went on to say that the building was used for storing coal, which was mined from down the pit. The shuffling of footsteps was then heard by two investigators coming from the bottom end of the Wagon Shop, and upon investigating these noises nothing untoward was found.

The rest of this vigil was rather quiet. Having said that, another group which was in this location earlier on, during their vigil, "sensed" a man and described him as having dirty, grubby blond hair. They also told us his name was Jack.

Jack had apparently shown her horrific injuries to his head, which he sustained during his physical life and, ultimately, had killed him. She then deduced this man had died following an accidental blow to the head with a pick. Upon checking the archives and records after the investigation, an entry states that a blow to the head from a pick killed a man named John Dinnery accidentally on 23rd

August 1919. It is also interesting to note that, back in those days, the name Jack was used as John and vice-versa!

We then headed to our final location for investigation, and this was the Blacksmiths' Workshop. It was now 3.45am, and we found this vigil to be very quiet indeed. The only interesting phenomenon documented was the constant flow and capture of orbs and light anomalies on the night-vision video camera. Asking the spirits to show themselves for us, or give us a sign to acknowledge their presence, proved rather fruitless. However, our team psychic, Glenn Hall, whilst in this location earlier on, picked up on the name "Thomas" and repeatedly sensed the date "1833" over and over again. Glenn then said he had to dig deeper to find the source of this information, only to be given the letter or initial B, and the image of people being suffocated in the dark. A possible explosion came to mind. Whilst checking the records and archives (again after the investigation), it was discovered that a young boy called Thomas Aisbett, eight years old, died in an explosion and was very likely suffocated underground. This, of course, would have been in the dark. The year was 1833. Could this have been the spirit who Glenn was picking up on and receiving the data from? It all seemed too much of a coincidence to me.

To summarise the investigation as a whole, I feel it started off rather well with different phenomena and activity being reported and documented. As the night wore on things seemed to settle down and the atmosphere became less physically active. What impressed me greatly was the data picked up by the team psychics, which are in fact documented in the museum archives and records; names, dates, events which our psychics could not have previously known due to the fact that these records are kept under lock and key and are not available to the public. This does indicate to me that the Bowes Railway museum is a very interesting investigation site and has a plethora of wonderful - but essentially harmless - ghosts, which are nothing more than residual energy and echoes from the past, recorded into the fabric of this wonderful place. I would like to thank our guest investigators and API founders Cindy Nunn and Jo Carnegie and our other guests for their invaluable assistance on this investigation.

Chapter Nine

Roman Ghosts Arbeia Roman Fort, South Shields.

Arbeia Roman Fort stands on the south side of the River Tyne in South Shields and is only four miles east the of Segedunum Roman fort and baths in what is now Wallsend. The earliest human occupation at Arbeia is thought to date back to 3000BC and, in the 3rd Century BC, an Iron age (800BC-AD 43) farm existed here. We know this because the remains of a burnt -down round-house was discovered and excavated in the south-east corner. The Roman fort at Arbeia, when it was originally built in around A.D.158, would have had a spectacular and commanding view across the estuary of the River Tyne, making it a very secure and well- defended settlement. It was home to approximately 600 Romans and its principal function was to act as a main gateway to the Roman Empire in Britain. It was also a garrison and military supply base for the Emperor Septimius Severus between AD 208-AD 210. After the death of Severus in AD 211, in

York, the fort remained a supply base and was used to serve the 17 forts along Hadrian's Wall (AD 122).

Between AD 222-AD 235 more accommodation was built for the entire garrison and, in the late third Century, the fort was laid siege to and burnt to the ground. During the rebuilding of the fort, two further Barracks were made to house the foot soldiers and in the South corner, a courtyard house was erected for the forts commanding officer.

By the early 400s the Roman Empire in Britain had declined and this period saw the arrival of the Anglo-Saxons (AD 410-AD 1069). Approximately 1000 years after the Roman abandonment of Arbeia it was re-discovered again in 1875 when the first archaeological excavations began. In 1949–1950 more excavations took place and uncovered the fort's perimeter boundaries. In 1953 an on-site museum was opened. In 1975 it became the property of *Tyne and Wear museums* and to this day, they preserve and care for this historic site. Furthermore they still carry out excavations and strive to uncover and learn more about Arbeia's hidden secrets of which I am sure there are many. For example, after recent excavations a number of bones and human remains were uncovered indicating that the fort at Arbeia may also be the site of one of the largest Roman burial grounds in the north east of England -just what the ghost hunters like.

In recent years the reconstruction of the West Gate, the barracks and the commanding officers courtyard house, gives people a chance to see how the Romans actually lived and worked. They rise from their original foundations and were built exactly the way they were in Roman times. Is it any wonder, that there have been so many ghost sightings in and around the fort? One story, which was related to me was that a certain homeowner who lives over the road from the site looked out of the window one night to see a Roman soldier silently walking about. It then disappeared behind one of the buildings and was not seen again.

Another case relates to the pub, which stands at the top of the street opposite the fort. The Look Out is alleged to be the host of a number of ghostly inhabitants, and one in particular is a spectral Roman legionnaire seen on a number of occasions in the pub cellar. Interestingly enough, research has shown that the actual cellar floor is on the same level as the Roman Fort, which stands over the road. It is also known the fort was a lot bigger than what we see today and it spans out in all four directions under the houses and shops and indeed under the Look Out pub itself. Perhaps the long-departed souls and spirits of the Roman Empire are to this day going about their duties unaware that they are now into the new millennium. It certainly seems to be the case. Interesting food for thought, don't you think?

On a pre-investigation visit when I was in the Commanding Officer's quarters I experienced what I believe to be my first paranormal - or at least odd - experience on this site. When I was trying to take a photo with my digital camera the shutter refused to go off when I pressed it. I tried once more to no avail, so I used my Nikon SLR 35mm that I had around my neck and, lo and behold, the shutter on that camera would not work either.

I lowered the camera and pressed the shutter and the shutter went off. (I now own a picture of the Commanding officers floor). One camera malfunction is odd, but two? It seems to me that someone did not want his or her photograph taken.

On the night of the 8th July 2005 *The North East Ghost In-Spectres* arrived to carry out their investigation. It was a lovely, warm night and there was no wind whatsoever, the air was still as could be. We arrived at 8pm and by 10.30pm we had begun the investigation. Trigger objects and lock-off video camera had been placed around the site and we started our surveillance in the Commanding Officer's house. For the first section of the investigation we all dressed up as Roman peasants in the hope any ghosts may interact more with us. It is a common theory that this technique seems to work on these investigations and as we found lots of old costumes in one of the rooms we thought we would give it a go.

It was not long into the investigation when Glenn Hall saw a blue, flashing light in the corridor of the Commanding Officer's house. A few minutes later I saw the exact same thing. The atmosphere then changed and the surrounding air went ice-cold, resulting in goose bumps and a sense of presence. We ventured to the section of the house where there are three bedrooms joined by a corridor and when we went to open the door which we had previously locked, we found the door open. (Two investigators present watched me actually lock the door earlier on and we had not returned to this room until then and the door was open). Upon entering these rooms the EMF meter showed no readings whatsoever and the rooms' temperatures were at a steady 18 degrees. We made our way in and sat down to listen and observe. At 11.15pm Suzanne McKay said she felt a cold rush of wind brush past her. Glenn felt this too but since I was on the other side of the room I felt nothing. The feelings of cold wind in these rooms proved to be commonplace as they were felt on two more occasions during this vigil, and as the air was still outside and there was no breeze at all as mentioned earlier on. It was a mystery as to where these bursts of cold air were coming from.

Both Suzanne and Glenn then detected a residual energy and they both agreed it was that of a young man, however no names were ascertained. We moved along into the next room to see if the presence that had been picked up would follow us along and it did. Dowsing with the rods indicated this as they pointed to where the spirit claimed to be when asked. Glenn and Suzanne also confirmed this by stating this spirit was standing in the doorway observing us. As nothing else happened for a while we decided to break before continuing the investigation. After our short break we ventured around to the other building block namely the Barracks. This is where in Roman times the foot soldiers would have slept. There are 5–6 rooms and they are very small indeed. Considering each room slept about 6–8 Roman soldiers conditions would have been very uncomfortable and cramped to say the least.

The trigger objects we placed in here earlier on had not moved at all and it seemed very quiet indeed. Although it was very dark and atmospheric, combined with the fact the quarters look original and authentic, you would expect this to be the ideal place to house ghosts and perhaps witness some activity. This was not the case so we moved our investigation to the West Gate area and our plan was to observe the ruined granaries and overlook the site from the top of the stairs. A mist rolled in from the North Sea giving the investigation a much needed and required ambient feel, which added to the whole experience. It was a typical and classical ghost-hunting scenario. Although this particular vigil proved fruitless too we will never forget the experience; it was eerie and atmospheric and it will be something I will never forget.

Since we were having good results in the Commanding Officer's house we decided to further our investigations in there and we returned to the bedrooms in which the presence was detected earlier. On entering we all felt as though we were being watched and a sudden chill came over us all. I called out into the atmosphere in the hope we got a response, and it was at this point Suzanne said she felt unwell and very uncomfortable indeed. At the same time Glenn then filmed a lovely light anomaly actually circling Suzanne. This footage must be seen to be believed. Another light anomaly was seen only by me this time, at the top of the room.

We decided to leave this room and venture into the Great Hall to check on a trigger object we had left in there. Earlier on when we placed the trigger object down we locked the door when we left. On returning we found yet again the door was open and unlocked. As with the other door, two investigators watched me lock this door and we can all testify we never returned until we found the door open. The trigger object had been moved too! It must be stressed that all team members were accounted for and trickery by others from outside can be eliminated too simply because they would have needed keys to get in thus indicating it would be some of the fort staff. I think not! And as we were the only people inside and we had locked ourselves in, it can only remain a mystery.

For our vigil in the Great Hall, we decided to go to our base room and get some small chairs to sit on as the only furniture in the hall, was part of the museum. Once more (and for the last time during the investigation) we found yet another previously-locked door unlocked. This was becoming quite a habit. The investigation in the Great Hall proved rather fruitless to say the least, and the Dictaphones and video cameras we had running in there during our vigil picked up no anomalies. But, all in all, still a fine investigation in a fabulous site; a site, which is no doubt one of the oldest, most historical sites in South Tyneside. Most haunted? I don't think so but I do feel it does have its share of resident spooks. Of that we are convinced.

I will leave you with one final proclamation. Unbeknown to us at the time, the doors in the Commanding Officer's house had been previously unlocking of their own volition and had been reported by fort staff on a number of occasions. We only found this out after the investigation when I relayed our experience to the fort staff.

Chapter Ten

G.H.O.S.T. in the Pub.
An anonymous Location
In Cumbria.

As well as being a member and founder of my own team
I also work with another research group called
GHOST (Ghosts & Hauntings Overnight Surveillance
Team). The team often investigate haunted properties
across the region and there is one investigation of many
that I have attended with GHOST that I would like to write
about in this section. However, due to the nature of the
haunting and the owners' concern regarding it, both parties
(myself and the owners) feel it is necessary to keep this
location a secret and their names will remain anonymous.

In the past few years or so, a ghost has been seen, inside
the property, emerging from a wall and slowly walking
along the bar area until he gets to a certain point in the
room. Then he simply disappears. He has been seen countless times by the pub owners and has also been sensed and
seen by visitors to the establishment.

The owners of this pub are obviously very distressed
and frightened by these episodes and called in the team in

the hope that we could give them some answers as to who the ghost is and why he his haunting their bar. We arrived at the location at about 11.00pm but did not get started until the early hours of the following morning. We split our team in two while one group went into room one upstairs and the other stayed downstairs in the bar. It was my group who ventured upstairs first and went into room one. The first thing we noticed was how cold the room was. By all accounts that room is always that cold and no matter what they do to try and heat it up, it remains cold! Anyway, we sat there for a while and just listened and observed.

I asked my colleague Lee Stephenson if he was drawn to anywhere in the room (as he gets certain feelings about certain places), and he told me he kept on focusing and looking at the door. This was odd to say the least, as that's where my eyes were being drawn too. Why? We don't know. I was trigger-happy with my digital camera while in this room and that in itself proved fruitful to say the least as I took a great photograph of what we believe is ghostly mist. When we purposely tried to reproduce this effect with our breath we could not! After a while, as nothing much was happening, we headed back downstairs for the first séance of the evening with the other team members, Drew Bartley and Fiona Vipond. The owners of this fine establishment also participated in this experiment.

At 02.46am the séance was started. After asking any presences to make themselves known to us, we all started to hear noises and movement coming from around the circle area. Light anomalies were caught on camera and a temperature drop was recorded in the middle of the circle. After a while it seemed to calm down a bit and then I was asked to lead the séance to see if a male voice would make the ghosts respond any better. We sat back down, all joined fingers on the table and I asked everyone present to focus on their breathing and uncross legs while keeping their feet flat on the floor. I then asked any spirits in the room if they would make themselves known to us. I then asked again but this time I addressed the ghost by his name, as through research carried out by our team researcher prior to the investigation (Drew Bartley), we believed we now had the name of this regularly seen apparition (which I must also keep anonymous).

"Mr X" I asked. "If you are here with us and can hear my voice and understand what I am saying please give us a sign".

I then asked if there were any more ghosts other than Mr X listening in, could they too make their presences known.

"Give us a knock or a rap, tap on something or touch someone, please let us know you are with us tonight".

It was at this point, to my front right and behind two of the sitters, I saw (or I thought I saw) a black shape with a human form. It was standing right in the spot where this ghost is said to come through the wall. I looked away frightened, and when I turned back around to see it, it was gone.

This actually happened twice during the séance. Knocks and bumps were also heard too throughout the proceedings and we all thought we heard the shuffling of ghostly feet.

The other amazing thing was that, as this séance was drawing to a close, the table tilted right off its feet and no one said they had done it. I asked them repeatedly and everyone was adamant they did not push or tilt the table nor move it back again. Then my arms and especially my thighs went bitter cold and I did not feel right. All of a sudden the table actually vibrated as though it was in an earth tremor and then it stopped. It vibrated once more before the close of the séance and it felt weird. Another sitter present also said his arms and thighs went bitter cold and he too felt the table vibrate twice. A good result.

We had a break for a while and, when we asked for the lights to be turned on, a bulb exploded with a bang and then the fan started to turn; even though we were told the fan was not switched on! Upon checking the trigger object, (which we placed earlier on) we found it had been moved about 5mm. *It is interesting to note that three individuals, who attended the séance, when asked what they thought, told me they were sitting in sceptic's corner. And after a bit of a chat one young lady in particular said the whole ghost thing and the séance was literally rubbish and she, or her colleagues, were not convinced.*

After our break we moved from the area of the first séance and sat in the other side of the bar for séance two. The idea being that the area in which the ghost is said to walk could be monitored properly while the séance was in progress. I ran the séance while the other team members monitored the area. I started the séance and almost straight away the proprietor's wife suffered immense hot and cold flushes while at the same time she wanted to cry one minute and then felt ok the next. This occurred all through-out the proceedings. I asked her if she was all right time and time again throughout the séance and each time she told me to continue. I think for her it was something she had never experienced before and it had a profound effect on her. This is where the séance took a turn. While I was asking Mr X to perhaps show himself, knocks and bumps, footsteps and shuffling were all heard in the area being monitored by Fiona Vipond. Lots of orbs were caught on digital camera and the more I asked for Mr X the more phenomena were being reported.

A massive temperature drop was then recorded with the laser thermometer gun. In the space of a minute and a half

66

the temperature dropped a staggering 14 degrees. Meanwhile in the circle the owner's wife was shivering cold and was almost weeping. Two of the sitters were now claiming to be able to see the ghost. It was pitch black and I think everyone was excited yet quite scared. I needed to be over in the bar area so without breaking the circle, I asked one of the sitters to continue with the séance while I ventured across. Fiona had been taken some stills with my camera, catching some good light anomalies; more strangely some red mist. She took a series of photographs and only one came out with the red mist. I had to ask her if she could have had a finger poised over the flash of the camera causing a possible red tint across the frame, as the light would have bounced of her finger giving this sort of effect but she was adamant that she took the photos the same way as the rest. So why did only one come up with this anomaly? Is it not also too much of a coincidence that this photo was taken at the precise time of all the other reported activity?

I must now refer the reader back to the sighting of the ghost by two sitters during the séance. The young lady who earlier was quoted in saying "It's all rubbish" was one of these sitters who claimed to see the apparition during the séance. As it turned out, after the séance ended she was shaken up badly, threw up violently in the toilets and then left the premises. A total sceptic had been converted, which in turn made the others think again as they left immediately after the séance too. So, after a very slow start to the night it turned out to be quite an interesting evening indeed. Lots of good activity was recorded and documented. Although only two areas in the whole building were investigated (Room One and the Bar), the results we got were quite astonishing to say the least. In regards to the apparition, we explained to the pub owners, because every time this ghost is seen it appears from out of the same wall and takes his walk along the bar area. He then disappears at exactly the same point every time, which leads us to the conclusion that this ghost is nothing more than a residual "stone tape" or place-memory apparition. I explained it poses no threat to them or their family whatsoever. He was happy with our diagnosis.

I think closure and understanding of the haunting of this establishment for the people who live there is a must. I now believe that they are on their way to understanding this particular haunting after the investigation and after we explained a few things to them. The residents of the establishment now seem a lot happier with the idea of what they have; or at least they now know the ghost or apparition they have is a harmless playback or psychic recording of nothing more than nice old gentleman who once resided there.

Chapter Eleven

A Touch of Spirit.
The Marsden Grotto
Pub, South Shields.

Believed by some to be the most haunted pub in Britain, the Marsden Grotto cave bar is a public house situated in the limestone cliffs in South Shields in Marsden Bay along the North East coast of England. It is on beach level and due to high freak tides it has often been flooded by the North Sea. It stands opposite the famous Marsden rock and its history dates back over two hundred years. The Marsden Grotto was made back in 1782 by a lead miner from Allenheads called Jack Bates who found himself unemployed and came to the area in search of work. He discovered the caves in the cliff face and, with his explosives; he blasted the caves into what they are today. That is why he is known historically as Jack the Blaster.

He and his wife Jessie lived in the home they made for the next ten years until Jack's death in 1792. The house was left abandoned and uninhabitable until 1826 when a man called Peter Allan renovated the derelict establishment and made it habitable once more. He named it The

Tam O' Shanter, but it was not long before it was renamed The Marsden Grotto. During his time there the smugglers of the day would often frequent the bay and this stretch of coastline and they became friendly with the landlord. They used the caves as a hideaway for themselves and their contraband.

Legend has it that in the 1840s a local HM customs man, out to catch these vagabonds, befriended a young smuggler. The smuggler soon cottoned on to what was happening and a fight broke out between the two. This resulted in the young rouge being shot and killed by the customs man. The smuggler's tankard was nailed up on the wall in the caves and it was said that if any man drinks from the tankard he would be cursed. It was also believed by the locals that should anyone move the tankard from the wall the establishment would also be cursed and the restless spirit of the young smuggler would horribly disturb any peace. It was from then on that the Grotto started to experience ghostly goings-on and paranormal activity. Objects would move around on their own. Dark shadows were often seen flitting around in the caves, and local legend has it that the smugglers tankard, when left on the bar at night with ale in, would mysteriously be empty in the morning. Some say it is the smuggler returning from the grave to drink his favourite ale from his favourite tankard as he did so often when he was alive.

It is also said that on stormy nights you can hear the screams of the tormented souls of the smugglers who died in the caves; those that lost their lives by either drowning in the freak high tides or were murdered by their so-called comrades.

In 1874 the establishment was taken over by Sidney Milnes Hawkes and, in 1898, the Vaux and Sons brewery leased the building only to take it over completely in 1938. To this day it is still a thriving pub and a wonderful drinking establishment, and the ghostly goings on are said to persist. Mysterious knocks and bumps are heard and there have been many ghost sightings. After an array of strange paranormal activity towards the end of 2004 the Grotto's [then] manageress called in *The North East Ghost In-Spectres* paranormal research team to investigate. We arrived on a cold November night to begin our series of investigations (19th November and 17th December 2004). Due to the Marsden Grotto being a thriving establishment we had to wait until the last of the punters vacated the premises, which they did at about 12.00 midnight.

It was then we began our investigation. We split up into our teams, and the investigation was underway. The family area and beer cellar was first for inspection and the first thing we all noticed was how cold this particular area was in comparison to the rest of the building. Although closed and locked fire doors were close by, we recorded a temperature drop of 5 degrees and it was getting even colder. We thought that there may have been a draught coming from these doors producing this temperature drop but tests proved there was no draught. Later on the temperature returned to its original reading, once more indicating the coldness was not and could not have been due to these fire doors.

So what was causing this cold spot? Around about the same time, Psychic Suzanne McKay was picking up on energy not far from where this temperature anomaly was recorded. She picked up on the spirit of a small boy who was called Samuel and she told us he was about 10 years old. She went on to say a blow to the head, probably from falling rocks from the nearby cliffs, had killed him. Suzanne also felt very weak at this point and said she could feel something stroking the back of her head.

It is interesting to add, that our other team psychic, Glenn Hall while in this very location later on in the investigation also picked up on a small boy called Samuel and he too complained of something touching the back of his head. Were these two names picked up and sensed by Suzanne and Glenn, one and the same spirit? The spirit of a young boy trapped as an earthbound soul aimlessly wondering and lingering at the scene of his horrific and sad death. Remember, before the building was built this spot would have been outside, and at the base of the cliffs. It was at this point I noticed movement in the form of a tall, dark figure near the bar area. When I went to investigate it, two other guest investigators came out from their location claiming to have heard footsteps and movement. Could there have been a connection with the movement I saw and the footsteps the two other investigators heard? As no one else was there I can only surmise (as the evidence points that way), that I saw the figure and they heard the footsteps of one of the many ghosts that this cave bar harbours. Very interesting and positive documentation of paranormal activity.

The next location for investigation was the small cave bar and the restaurant upstairs. The first odd happening was that upon arrival into this location I and another investigator felt an ice-cold blast of air rush past us and we could not work out where it came from. Light anomalies and orbs were recorded and caught on night vision video camera and our tests proved these were not caused by any normal means such as torchlight or camera flashes.

All very interesting to say the least but one of the strangest things I have ever seen on our investigations happened when I walked into the restaurant area. The North East Ghost In-Spectres team psychic Suzanne McKay was sitting down against the wall with her eyes closed when all of a sudden I saw a white mist come out from the front of her face and rise up into the air then completely disappear. I called her name and she came around with a start. She then told me she was trying to contact a spirit and this spirit had got way to close to her, and was beginning to take her over. She was quite shaken up by this episode. Whatever happened to Suzanne I will probably never know for sure, but I know what I saw and it was incredible.

We then based ourselves back in the small bar area. Then came the sighting of a misty white apparition of just a torso and a head. A writer and reporter and good friend of ours from the South Shields Gazette, who I invited with us to write the article for local newspaper, saw this ghost apparition. It was described as a woman of about 60–70 years old, thin in stature with grey hair and a gaunt face. She was also reported to have on a frilly garment of clothing. This sighting happened quite quickly and was reported to have floated past the bottom of the thin stairwell we were sitting at the top of. When I asked if anyone could get a name for this lady I was given Josie by one of the team psychics.

It is a tantalising thought that this ghost could have been the wife of Jack Bates as she is said to haunt this particular area of the Grotto. Not only that but the description given to us fits that of Jack's wife and, more so, her name is Jessie. Unfortunately no one else saw this apparition and although a sighting would have been better by two or more investigators, I trust the testimony of the researchers and guests 110%. Furthermore the details given correlate with the historical records. Along with muttering and disembodied voices and movement being reported later on in this investigation, this location proved to be very active indeed.

To continue with the investigation our next location was the large cave bar, but before we went into this location another group had already been in here earlier on in the evening and had allegedly made contact with a spirit.

This spirit had by all accounts, been showing the group some interesting phenomena such as temperature drops and light anomalies and was asked by a guest psychic if he could give the next group in here (us) a definite sign to acknowledge his presence. Unknown to us, he said he would. When we went into the cave area, the brand-new batteries used for the video camera and torches drained of energy almost straight away. Suzanne McKay then picked up the essence of a man situated near the cave wall next to the security light in the south end of the cave. In the exact same spot later on in our vigil another investigator said she saw a figure of a man standing upright with his hands clasped behind his back. She told us he was a bouncer type of fellow with white gloves on. He was standing side on to the investigator and then he just disappeared.

It was at this point the security light on the wall, went out altogether. By law these lights should stay on all the time, and when we asked if we could turn them off for the investigation, we were refused. I wondered if any other strange phenomena were being reported elsewhere on the investigation at this point, and when I found the [then] manageress (Sue Birkbeck), she informed me all the security lights had went out and she did not know why. Nobody had touched them and upon inspection we found that these particular security lights were still connected up and switched on. The next ten minutes or so were utter pandemonium as other lights that were unplugged came on, and lights that should have been on mysteriously went out. One set of lights came on although they were not even connected up to the mains. It was also noticed that the CCTV monitor was flicking on and off. Was this the sign and verification of presence that the guest psychic had asked for prior to our vigil in there? He seemed to think so, and it all seemed like too much of a coincidence to me. We were also informed after the investigation, all the lighting went back to normal and further tests proved there was nothing wrong with the electrics.

So, a very eventful night to say the least. A whole host of evidence documented and collated. The team psychics and guest psychics were fantastic as always, and picked up on lots of data and information, which was historically accurate. Then there was the actual phenomenon, which was witnessed by all present on the investigation in regards to the lighting disturbances near the end of the investigation. Three alleged spectres were reported to have actually been seen in different parts of the establishment, this along with all the other phenomena recorded, has convinced me that this pub, as stated in the beginning of this chapter, could well be the most haunted pub in Britain.

An infrared image of the magnificent keep at Warkworth.

Bamburgh Castle in Northumberland as the sun sinks. Said to be haunted by a grey lady.

The building in Dieppe, France where I experienced terrifying poltergeist phenomena.

The haunted house where I lived as a boy.

The spot on the old railway line where I heard the crunching of footsteps behind me as a youngster on my way home. Now Hadrian's Way.

A classic orb, said to be the first stages of ghost materializations.

An enhancement of the orb.

Modern day ghost hunting equipment.

Byker Community centre.

The Schooner Hotel.

The Bowes Railway Museum.

Arbeia Roman Fort.

Anonymous Location in Cumbria.

The Marsden Grotto Pub.

Newcastle Keep

The Haunted Cockpit.

Harperley POW Camp.

The Manorhouse in Ferryhill.

The GHOST Investigation Team.

The El- Coto Restaurant, Newcastle.

The El-Torero Restaurant, Newcastle.

The Coroner's Court Building, Newcastle Quayside.

Newcastle Garth. Our venue for the charity investigation.

An anonymous location in Durham.

Rachel Lacy, York's Ghost-finder general, the author, writer Mike Hallowell, ITVs Haunted Homes Mark Webb, and Vision magazine editor and medium, Diana Jarvis.

The Author, Darren W Ritson.

Chapter Twelve

To keep vigil.
Newcastle Keep,
Newcastle upon Tyne

As far back as historical records show it is believed the first fortification built on the site of the Newcastle Garth belonged to the Roman Empire in 120 AD. In those days the fortress was called Pons Aelius and it was essentially built to safeguard and defend the bridge called Pons Aelii, which was also built by the Romans and stood roughly where the Swing Bridge now stands.

It is believed that some time later an ancient Anglo-Saxon burial ground occupied the site and modern day archaeology has proved this to be so. Around 1,000 years later the eldest son of William The Conqueror, Robert Curthose, built another fortress in 1080 on the same site with wood and earth. In the 1100s, in the reign of Henry II, it was constructed again from sandstone. The stone castle took five years (1172 - 1177) to build, at around a cost of £1000.

This is what we see today and it is a fine illustration of the late Norman workmanship.

The Castle's primary objective, as was Pons Aelius, was the protection and defence of Newcastle, and as the site in which it was built is on high ground overlooking and dominating the valley, it was inevitable that the fort would be built in this spot. Nowadays its dominating position has been hidden by modern edifices, which have been developed around it.

After almost 1000 years of sieges, invasions and bloody warfare, the castle was used as a common gaol, and for two hundred years rapists, murderers, thieves and all kinds of petty criminals were held there, under the most disgusting, cramped and squalid conditions. As you can imagine, sanitation was poor and disease was rife for the overcrowded inmates and many deaths occurred due to these conditions. One of the castle's more famous or better-known inmates was William Winter. He was allegedly held here after his trial at the Moot Hall before he was hanged in 1792 at Westgate in Newcastle.

William Winter murdered an old lady called Margaret Crozier in August 1791 in a place called Elsdon, which is about 20 miles east of Otterburn in Northumberland. His lifeless body was then taken to the scene of his crime where it was hung up in a gibbet cage as a deterrent to other would-be criminals. It is said that he haunts this lonely, barren and cold moor, longingly looking on from the roadside and staring at his gibbet post. Could William Winter also haunt the bowels of the keep where once he was held as a prisoner? The gibbet post still stands to this day up on the moors at Elsdon and is known as "Winter's Gibbet" or "The Elsdon Gibbet" and has a wooden head that hangs from it. It is an eerie chilling sight that would unnerve the most sceptical of people should they stumble across it one foggy or misty evening.

Nowadays the Castle Keep is a popular museum and is owned by the Society of Antiquities, as is the Black Gate,

which stands opposite. It is also the oldest and most historical building in Newcastle, so you can understand why this
particular building was a *must* place to investigate. During
the past few years or so, I have investigated and took part
in no less than twelve investigations with other research
teams and ghost-hunters from the region and encountered
what I believe to be good paranormal phenomena. On one
occasion I saw a black shadow pass by the window and
block out the light at the top of the stairs in the mezzanine
chamber. This was accompanied by the shuffling of footsteps and, upon inspection; no one else was in the vicinity.
Others also witnessed this occurrence.

On another occasion I heard a long drawn-out sigh
coming from the empty Garrison Room and heard a
disembodied muttering right in my ear while standing
alone in the Queen's Chamber. This muttering was accompanied by breath on my ear and neck. This I feel is
evidence that I personally cannot dispute.

The account you will now read is taken from the two
investigations planned and conducted by *The North East
Ghost In-Spectres.* The two investigations were held
approximately within 6 months of each other. Our first
visit to the Castle was on 30th October running in to the
31st October 2004, and one question was on my mind:
"Would Halloween make a difference to our investigation?" Well, we would find out soon enough because, at the
stroke of midnight, as we ran into All Hallows Eve, we
held a séance in the Great Hall and it proved rather interesting to say the least. As midnight struck and the bells
from Newcastle Cathedral rang out, we were all in a circle
holding hands and attempting to communicate with the
spirits of the Keep. During these proceedings it was
reported that one investigator felt a constant, warm breath
on the back of his neck although no one was physically
behind him. It was also reported that two other investiga-

tors had the chains around their necks pulled and tugged upon by unseen hands. More interestingly, one investigator (who shall remain nameless) claimed to have seen a bright, white mist in human form passing the doorway to the Great Hall as if it were heading up the stairwell to the galleries. So, all in all, an interesting start to the investigation. It was after this séance we split into our groups to cover more of the castle. I will now briefly summarise the rest of this particular investigation.

During the course of the investigation various temperature drops were recorded along with cold spots. At one point I actually felt something touch the side of my face although no one was near me at the time. Also, EMF anomalies were recorded in abundance along with photographic evidence of light anomalies making this investigation a very interesting one indeed.

Another séance was held at 5am, only this time in the Garrison Room and former prison. The séance lasted for 45–50 minutes and there were five sitters and one observer. This séance was quite productive and reports were coming in that sitters were being touched and prodded whilst, simultaneously, the room temperature dropped dramatically. The most interesting part of these proceedings was actually hearing footsteps and the shuffling of feet coming from outside the Chapel area. We could all clearly here these footfalls from inside the garrison room and when an investigator went to take a look, no one was there. Not a bad night's work; maybe running the investigation into Halloween was not such a bad idea after all, who knows?

Our second investigation took place on April 9th 2005. It was a warm and clear night, and as usual we split into our teams and headed off into the castle and it was not long before the occurrences began. One of our guest investigators for the night, while in the Well Room, photographed an anomalous mist as the temperature dropped from 20 degrees to 14 degrees.

An interesting start! I called out to the atmosphere and asked if the spirits present would acknowledge us in any way, and at that precise time another photograph showing anomalous mist was taken.

At 12.30am a séance was held in the galleries in the upper section of the castle overlooking the Great Hall. It was reported earlier on that a woman in an old, white dress was seen by two researchers in the vicinity. (This is not the first time investigators have reported a presence of a woman up here, as other ghost-hunting teams from the region have this phenomenon documented as I found out after our investigation). Our séance unfortunately proved rather fruitless and nothing with any good evidential value was recorded or documented.

It is now 1.00am and we are in the Garrison Room. A musty smell hits us all in the face; what it is we do not know. After a few minutes in there, myself and another investigator both clearly hear a long drawn-out breath or sigh emanating from a part of the room in which no one stood. (Or was there?) This occurrence is a regular thing down in the old prison. Could these sighs be the echoes from the past of the former prisoners and criminals who were once held in this very room awaiting certain death? It's a tantalising thought. We ventured through to the Chapel and this time we were greeted by a nice, sweet smell of what can only be described as incense and this was the only documented oddity during our vigil in this location. The hours passed, and it all seemed to be quieting down until we had another séance downstairs in the Garrison Room. It was lead by The *North East Ghost In-Spectres* team psychic Suzanne McKay as we all stood in a big circle around the pillar and held hands. I asked

Suzanne to ask if the spirit of William Winter was, in actual fact, with us.

A few positive responses were documented. Three video cameras, two of which were set up on tri-pods, turned themselves off completely with no one near them. A black figure was seen inside the circle moving around. I know this to be true because it was I who saw it. It was at this point that Suzanne McKay came over and stood behind me, which was fortunate as we were both party to witnessing some of the most frightening phenomena of the night. As the séance was commencing I looked up to my front right corner only to see a black mass of dark energy coming towards me over the tops of the heads of the other circle members. It came at some speed and, as it approached, I broke the circle and ducked to avoid it. When I composed myself it had gone.

Could I have actually stopped this thing in its tracks due to the fact I broke the circle and the energy it had somehow created? I cannot help thinking this was the case. I would have thought I was going mad had it not been for Suzanne also seeing this black mass from where she was standing directly behind me. During this pandemonium three, loud knocks were heard on the closed Garrison Room door and we all thought it was the castle warden coming down to see what the noise was. It was not. On opening the door no one was there. The séance and the investigation ended at 4.30am and it has to be one of the most remarkable investigations I have run to date. The old Keep at Newcastle is without question a hive of paranormal activity and in my opinion the Garrison Room has to be the most haunted location in there. So just remember, the next time you are visiting this wonderful museum and you suddenly feel anxious or unnerved for some reason, or perhaps it becomes a great deal colder, beware; you may not be on your own.

Chapter Thirteen

Plane Old Ghosts A 1952 Canberra Bomber Cockpit.

In early March of 2005, a fellow paranormal investigator and newspaper columnist who informed me of a haunting of the more unorthodox kind contacted me. He explained to me one of his readers had contacted him in the hope of getting some help and advice on a possible ghost he thought he had. My acquaintance went on to explain that this fellow was in possession of an old 1954 B2 Canberra bomber and claimed the actual cockpit of the aeroplane was haunted. As my acquaintance was very busy with his writing and other work commitments he referred the case to *The North East Ghost In-Spectres*. I was given the telephone number of the owner of the bomber and phoned him up for a chat.

This particular Canberra B2 bomber was built in 1954 by Hadley Page and primarily used for photographic reconnaissance flights, although it was used in 1956 as part of Upwoods Bomber Wing. In 1993 the aircraft was dismantled and reduced to the cockpit section, which in turn went to Liverpool in the same year and stayed there until 2001. It was then purchased by the NAHM group at Hooton Park in Wirral until it fell into the hands of aircraft enthusiast and cockpit restoration expert, Karl Edmondson.

The first thing he told me on the telephone was that he was a total sceptic when it came to ghosts and the paranormal, but was willing to keep an open mind. He went on to explain that he had been taking photographs inside his cockpit and had captured some strange orbs or light anomalies. At that point in time he did not know what these were, nor did he even notice them on the pictures until a colleague of his pointed them out to him. As it happens he knew of someone who claimed to be psychic and, out of sheer curiosity, asked her to check out the cockpit. This she did and she came up with details and names, which were historically accurate, much to the owner's surprise when he researched it. From a total sceptic to a man now very much intrigued, he now wanted to know more.

We arranged a day to go over and visit the cockpit, and on the 26th March 2005, myself and *The North East Ghost In-Spectres* team psychic Suzanne McKay arrived at the hanger to conduct a preliminary baseline investigation. As the owner of the cockpit wanted answers the first thing we would need to know was what type of ghost this cockpit was supposed to have. After an EMF sweep which showed no anomalies whatsoever, and after a few photographs were taken, I decided to place Suzanne in the cockpit for a while and see if she could pick anything up psychically from inside. To briefly summarise, the afternoon's preliminaries produced some interesting results. Suzanne picked up on an energy, which was indeed residual, and we came to the conclusion there were no active spirits in the cockpit.

The energy picked up was a benevolent warm energy left over from bygone times as the cockpit has merely retained some events and happenings and has been recorded into the fabric of the actual plane nose, however some anguish and pain was also picked up too. Interestingly enough, just before we left I took a single frame photograph inside the cockpit and caught what looks like to be, a long light anomaly in movement. I then swept the area with my EMF meter precisely where this anomaly was caught, and, lo and behold, I had an anomalous reading, which was fluctuating between 4 and 10 milligauss, which in paranormal terms is very interesting indeed. On taking a photo of the plane from outside I again caught another orb. The interesting thing regarding this photo was that when taking pictures outside in a certain light, my camera flash does not go off, as was the case in this instance. Therefore I feel this eliminates the theory that this particular orb is a result of a reflection from a dust particle. So, what could this one be?

On the night of 27th May 2005 *The North East Ghost In-Spectres* turned up at Bowes Railway Museum, where the cockpit was kept for the night, to conduct the full investigation. There is only so much you can do with a small investigation like this one so the plan was to put investigators into the cockpit separately and at different times during the night and ask them to report any strange occurrences or impressions and write them down. The notes and information collated (as always) would be kept quiet and separate, and comparisons would be made at the end of the investigation to see if any similar occurrences took place. We started the investigation with the cockpit around 11.00pm and our team psychic Suzanne McKay went in first to conduct a vigil.

The first thing she reported was that she caught a glimpse of a shadow moving about inside the cockpit. She then felt dizzy and picked up the names "Albert Smith", a "Thomas" aged 33 and a man called "Jackson" aged 46.It was then reported that a murmuring was heard either inside or just outside the cockpit; no one was outside the cockpit at the time so we can only surmise it was inside. (This too was heard later on during another investigator's sitting). Karl Joined Suzanne for a brief period inside the cockpit and saw what he claims to be a white blur move across Suzanne's chest. It was at this point that Suzanne picked up Albert Smith's middle name, which she told us was Stuart. He was apparently 28–29 years old and died of a heart attack in the cockpit. (It must be stressed that I too felt pains in my chest while sitting in the back seat and thought of a heart attack). Karl and Suzanne both then heard the sound of what can only be described as a crisp packet being crumpled up. What it was remains a mystery to this day.

Claire Smith then takes vigil in the cockpit and, when asking out for phenomena, a strap hanging up inside starts to move and sway. She also picks up the feeling of deafness for a while and later said her ears popped and went muffled. She also felt a pressure in her head which begs the question, could she be picking up on what would happen if the pressure was affecting her ears as if it would when in flight? It certainly is a tantalising thought indeed. Claire then reported that her camera would not take photos, which is common in alleged haunted places and on coming out the cockpit the camera seemed to work just fine. What is also very interesting is that she also got the number 12 going over in her head. As it turns out the plane, when in use, joined number 12-group Commanders' Flight at RAF Colerne before being re-classified as a ground instructional airframe with No 12 School of Technical Training at RAF Melksham.

Next up was another site investigator. He took vigil inside the cockpit, and had a profound experience whilst in there. He claims to have heard murmuring emanating from within the cockpit and then went all dizzy and disorientated and felt as though he was moving down a tunnel. It could be said that this experience has a psychological and rational explanation which of course the team keeps an open mind to, but nevertheless it shook this investigator up quite badly and he had to shake himself round and was quite disturbed about the whole thing. His torch batteries, which were put in brand new, then quickly drained of energy thus dimming his torchlight. Again, this often happens in paranormal investigations.

It was now proving to be a rather interesting investigation and we wondered what other phenomena may be experienced, so we locked off a night vision video camera and a Dictatation machine in the cockpit for one hour to see if we could pick up on any hard evidence of paranormal activity. The results are quite startling. What sounds like faint beeping can be heard on the cassette along with the occasional clear click or tapping noise. Could it be the workings and switches being flicked and played with by a resident phantom pilot? On night vision video camera we captured a number of good light anomalies or orbs, floating aimlessly around the cockpit, also indicating an energy may be recorded into the cockpit. But the best was yet to come.

On the dictation machine cassette about 25 minutes into the recording you can clearly hear knocks and bumps as if there is someone moving about inside the empty cockpit, and of course there was not! They started very quiet and faint and built up to loud distinct bumps and bangs. One investigator likened then to a coughing sound but I am not too sure. Nevertheless it was a good result, and very odd indeed. In total we counted about 15–20 knocks and bumps coming from inside the empty plane nose.

So the investigation was then at an end and I feel we did all what we could do. The results were not bad at all. A trigger object of a navigator's protractor that we drew around and left earlier on had not moved at all, but the dictation machine recordings, the video-taped light anomalies and the phenomena witnessed by both Karl and Suzanne were truly amazing.

Along with the murmuring heard by two investigators at different times, and the two investigators feeling dizziness at different times is also of significance to the investigation. There are also the knocks and bumps clearly heard on a locked off cassette, and all of the other documented phenomena, including a good photograph of an anomalous mist floating around the plane nose. This can only lead us to conclude that there may well be a residual energy or some sort of echo from the past recorded into the fabric of the cockpit and for such a small and tiny cockpit I feel the results were quite astounding to say the least. It must also be said that there is nothing untoward or malevolent at all, and what we have is a friendly and benevolent energy that from time to time replays over what once happened in days gone by.

Chapter Fourteen

Eternally Captive. Harperley Prisoner of War Camp, Fir Tree, Co Durham.

Invited as guests on the 30th July 2005 by API (Anomalous Phenomena Investigations), *The North East Ghost In-Spectres* ventured up to Weardale near County Durham to investigate the former World War II prisoner-of-war camp.

The prison camp at Harperley was actually built by Italian prisoners in the early 1940s that were held there and housed in tents. They built the prefabricated huts that stand today and it was these huts that went on to house German prisoners of war. In comparison to most POW camps, this camp at Harperley was known for the hospitality, kindness and the well-being of all the prisoners held captive during these times. Although they were worked extremely hard, these prisoners were treat with respect, fed well and looked after. They were also allowed to indulge in pass-times such as gardening and painting, and some of their original works of art can still be seen today hanging up in some of the huts.

Out of the 60 huts that originally occupied this site, 50 now remain and a number of them have recently been restored. The rest are awaiting restoration. There is also a chapel and a theatre with a built in orchestra pit, and this was used by the prisoners for putting on shows and entertainment. This theatre was also used as a cinema.

It is now open to the public as a museum and people can visit the camp, step back in time and be presented with the World War II POW camp experience. This POW camp has now been classed as an ancient monument by English Heritage and has been recently featured on the BBC as part of the *Restoration* programme. So, how could *The North East Ghost In-Spectres* team refuse such a tantalising offer to spend the night in such a historic and allegedly haunted location such as this? We had to oblige and go along. After all, which self-respecting ghost hunter wouldn't?

On the night we were also joined by members of Team Phenomena (ran by our very own Suzanne McKay) and Otherworld North East, who also relished this great opportunity given to us by the API team. We arrived at 9.30pm and were treated to a half-hour documentary about life as a prisoner back in WWII. This was narrated by a former prisoner, telling people all about his experiences and his life as a prisoner of war. After the short documentary we were split into four groups and we headed off into the night to investigate the POW camp. Our first location was hut 22 and the time was 11.00pm. The first thing we all noticed was how oppressive the atmosphere was and we all got the impression we were being watched from the outside. The preliminary temperature and EMF sweeps showed no anomalies. The air outside was normal and there was no wind or breezes at this point in the investigation. We sat and observed for a while until an Otherworld North East Member started to ask the spirits for phenomena. It was then reported that a scratching noise was heard coming from inside the hut. Rats or mice? A sudden burst of cold wind then swept across the room but one has to take into account this hut was open to the elements as it had no windows in, and neither did it have any doors. However, as stated earlier the night was calm at this present time, so who knows?

This first vigil was interesting because of light anomalies being seen with the naked eye by all members of the group, and there were indeed a few seen. What feelings each and every member of the group experienced. Feelings of dizziness, headaches, tired, heavy legs and "jelly legs" were all mentioned by the group.

One auditory phenomenon that was witnessed was that of a loud, distinct thump, or footstep, which two of the investigators heard clearly. So, not a bad start to the night, but it all pales in comparison as what happened to me whilst on a break in between vigils.

At 12.30am, while standing outside of hut 13 near the base room, I was chatting to colleagues when I become aware of a figure out of the corner of my eye. At first I thought it was an investigator and, when I turned to look, I realised it was not an investigator for it then proceeded to move forwards and straight into the back of a tractor that happened to be parked in its path. It simply vanished before my eyes. All I could ascertain was that it was a clear figure of a man and it was, I believe, a ghost apparition. Obviously the ghost would not have been aware of the tractor that was parked there and that is why he walked through the back of it. I was dumfounded for a minute or two, simply because I saw the ghost in the first place, and it was when I least expected to. Was this the ghost of a former German prisoner or could it have been a British soldier? Who knows for sure; but whoever he is, he's unfortunate to be held captive there for all eternity. It was a fabulous sighting for my part but unfortunately I was the only one to witness it. I excitedly told everyone present and asked the event organisers (Cindy and Colin Nunn) if there had been any recorded sightings in that area or any data in the records to back up my sighting. Rest assured, I am not lying nor am I mistaken in what I saw. It is this fact that makes this particular investigation one I will never forget. I had not seen a ghost with crystal clarity like this since I was a small boy and, after 55 investigations, this was the best paranormal activity I have witnessed.

Moving on with the investigation, we then proceeded to hut 13 in the camp and again the EMF sweep showed no anomalous readings, so we just sat and waited. Some rod and crystal dowsing was attempted and the spirit of a man claiming to be a prisoner of war came through, but only momentarily. He acknowledged his presence and then he was gone. Could this be the man who appeared in shadow form to an investigator earlier on in the evening? The possibility is there. The earlier group's dowsing indicated that he did show himself, and when asked to point into the area with the rods as to where he showed himself, sure enough the rods pointed to where the investigator saw it. This was done, of course, without the dowsers knowledge of what had happened and I feel it does add credence to the sighting and of course the validity of rod dowsing.

Soon the sound of men murmuring was heard by API member Jo, and no one in the vicinity could be heard. It remains a mystery. For most of this vigil I must admit I spent the time looking out the window to where the tractor stood, for this location was nearby, hoping for another brief glimpse of the ghost I saw earlier on in this area. Unfortunately I saw him no more, and deep down, I knew this would be the case.

The other groups on the investigation were also subject to phenomena deemed as unexplainable. *The North East Ghost In-Spectres'* Darren Olley had an experience he too will not forget, and being level-headed and sceptical of ghosts at this point, he finds this episode very hard to explain away. While investigating hut 13 he claims to have seen a shadow of a man standing right in front of him and, aware that the rest of the group was in another part of hut 13, he knew it was not them. When he looked again it was gone. So what, or who, did he see? Were his eyes playing tricks in the dark? I guess we will never know for sure. Temperature drops, moving shadows, light anomalies caught on camera, feelings of nausea and sickness and the unmistakeable sound of an old gramophone record being heard along with my own ghost sighting leads me to believe this may be one of the most haunted sites I have investigated to date. My thanks go to Cindy and Colin Nunn and Jo and Chris Carnegie for Inviting *The North East Ghost In-Spectres* to this wonderful location and giving us this great opportunity. Harperley prisoner of war camp is open to the public and is well worth a visit. With gift shops, restaurant, play area for children, guided tours and much more this one time prison is now a great museum and a fabulous day out. I recommend you all pay a visit.

Chapter Fifteen

Kids will be Kids The Manor House Hotel, Ferryhill, Co Durham.

The Manor House in Ferryhill lies approximately Seven miles south of Durham. It dates back to the sixteenth century where it began its life as a farmer's dwelling. In 1642 John Wilkinson sold it to John Shawe, and when he died it passed to his grandson Ralph. By the early 1700s the house and surrounding land had seen many more owners and, by 1885, only the house remained as the land had been sold on to the local colliery. In 1891 the house was fully restored and occupied by Henry Palmer. Since 1891 it has been occupied by many more people. In 2001 a family bought the premises and turned the Manor House into a thriving hotel, which is open to this day.

This 16th Century one-time orphanage, Manor House and now hotel is reputedly haunted by a number of ghosts and spirits that once dwelt on this land. A ghost of a woman is said to walk the stairwell inside the premises looking for her baby, aimlessly wondering around in torment. It is also said the bones of children were found buried in the grounds of the building, signifying possible murders and cover-ups. Rooms 7 and 8 have also been subject to extremely violent poltergeist activity and ghostly apparitions resulting in the absolute terror of the present owners. Two prior investigations and two failed attempts at exorcism in an effort to end the hauntings, or at least understand them, has led the hauntings to become even worse and we are very lucky indeed to have been able to carry out an investigation.

On Saturday the 17th Sept 2005 the G.H.O.S.T Investigation team (of which I am a team member) and a few selected guests carried out an investigation and it has to be another one of the best I have attended to date as a ghost hunter. We arrived at about 8.30pm on the night in question and were shown to the most haunted wing of the building; rooms 7 and 8. We made ourselves comfortable and prepared for the night's investigation. As always some preliminary baseline tests were carried out before the investigation and one or two anomalies were indeed picked up. A temperature drop of 4 degrees was recorded while carrying out the tests and both myself and Drew Bartley's EMF meter recorded very high readings over both of the beds in room 8. They were there one minute, gone the next. Room 7 and the adjoining corridors showed no anomalous readings and the temperature averaged around 20 degrees in the bedrooms and 25 degrees in the corridor.

We set up a trigger object in room 7 and a flour tray experiment in room 8. A long, plastic tub of flour was placed on a sturdy surface and objects were placed into the flour. In this case we used crystals and a red lollipop as young spirit children allegedly frequent this area. By placing these objects into the tray and leaving the crucifix locked off in room 7, we hoped we might achieve some spiritual interaction with these objects; ultimately they may be moved indicating some form of ghostly activity. We then split into two groups and while myself, Lee Stephenson, Suzanne McKay and Fiona Vipond went to room 8 to investigate, Drew Bartley and his group stayed in room 7. Our investigation began with us settling down, calling out to the atmosphere and asking for phenomena while at the same time recording it with my dictation machine. For a while nothing seemed to happen until quite a while into the vigil when we all started to hear the odd click, or tap. Some investigators also felt funny feelings, and the distinct smell of sick was smelt by all at one point in the vigil; a commonly reported occurrence.

After the split vigils we all regrouped back in room 8, where earlier on it had been reported that the beam barriers that were placed at the door had been turned around while the investigators were all sitting on the bed. It was here we decided to hold a séance. This, it seemed was the room to investigate thoroughly. We caught some light anomalies on the night vision video camera and there was a definite feeling of something or someone around us, this was agreed by all present.

Drew and myself monitored the séance proceedings while the rest of the group sat in the circle and conducted the séance. Prior to the séance beginning, a photograph was taken of the flour tray showing ten crystals, a red lollipop, and flat, undisturbed floor. When everyone was ready and comfortable, Suzanne McKay (*The North East Ghost In-Spectres* team psychic) proceeded to conduct the séance and it wasn't long before she was aware of spirit presences. She picked up on two children, a boy and a girl and said they were related. The children were then asked if they would like a lollipop and were told that they were welcome to take the one we had left as a trigger object in the flour.

After a minute or so, I shone my torch onto the flour tray to see if there had been any movement with our objects and I was not disappointed. I had noticed that the flour had indeed been disturbed, as if someone had literally dragged 2 or 3 their fingers through the flour leaving it piled up at one side of the tray. But then the real shock came as we then noticed the red lollipop had completely vanished from within the tray! I was monitoring the séance from that area so I know no one had touched it. Drew Bartley was on the other side of the room and everyone else was sitting in the séance. So who took the lollipop? It is not hard to work out it was one of the spirit children.

This was a first for us all, for all the trigger object experiments we have set up over the years, some do indeed move from their positions but only slightly or an inch at the most, but this one had completely vanished and was taken away from under all our noses and was never seen again. I can assure you, no one touched the flour tray objects and everyone turned out their pockets and was checked for flour on their hands and clothes just as a precautionary measure, and everyone was clean, but we knew this would be the case. It is also interesting to add that flour patches and flour stains were later found on the carpet near the room door, (this patch was the identical size and shape of the lollipop); we also found flour in the bathroom, outside on the landing and down the stairs in the corridor. We can only conclude it was taken from the flour tray by the children, out of the room, into the corridor and down the stairs after all, we all know that no one living had left the room while we were there. This incident baffled us all and we were all convinced we had experienced ghostly activity. We were so impressed we spent the rest of the night talking it through and trying to locate the lollipop stick. We never found it.

So, what a night of investigating we had. It certainly proved very interesting indeed and some of the best results were ascertained to date. Although the malevolent entity that is also said to reside in room 8 did not manifest for us in the way we had hoped, the spirit children really did us proud. So if you ever decide to book into room 8 at the Manor House in Ferryhill, and if you have a sweet tooth, keep your eyes on your confectionary.

Chapter Sixteen

Serving up some spirit. The El-Coto Spanish Restaurant, Newcastle upon Tyne

The *El-Coto* Spanish restaurant is situated in the centre of Newcastle upon Tyne on Leazes Park Road and stands opposite the magnificent 1880 John Johnson's synagogue. It is thought that David Stephenson designed Leazes Park Road around 1811, and it was originally named Albion Place, the continuation of Albion Street. It is believed that in-between 1896 and 1914 the name was changed to Leazes Park Road. 21 Leazes Park Road, the site of the *El-Cotto* restaurant, has a rich and varied history dating back to at least 1811 with a whole host of people having resided, worked and lived at this location.

Although the area is called Gallowgate, it is believed that the Newcastle gallows were situated elsewhere. However, it is rumoured that hangings did indeed take place on the site of this restaurant, specifically in the adjacent

119

courtyard. One hanging is believed to have taken place in the front of the building. Over the years the property has seen many faces come and go, ranging from grocers, insurance agents, cabinet makers and joiners, sofa manufacturers, a gunsmith and solicitors to name but a few. It has been used as a private dwelling, a business to trade and for commerce and is now currently a thriving city centre restaurant.

I think 21 Leazes Park Road has seen it all. It is not surprising that the area - and this particular property - is reputed to be haunted by a number of ghosts and spirits. Lost souls wondering aimlessly around the property in search of peace? Or ghosts who once resided here and liked the place so much they did not want to depart? This is what the owners and staff of *El-Coto* have been asking themselves over the past few months after a series of inexplicable happenings. Dark figures have been seen moving about the place, mysterious knocking is heard coming from the passage windows when no one is around, footsteps in empty rooms are often heard and, more chillingly, it was reported that a member of staff ventured upstairs on his own to the upper restaurant and sensed he was being followed. He stopped in his tracks and then heard a voice directly behind him. When he turned around, no one was there. He was the only person in that wing of the building at this particular time, and by all accounts was terrified.

So who or what is causing the disturbances at 21 Leazes Park Road? *The North East Ghost In-Spectres* research team was called in to investigate after the owner contacted us. Fascinated and intrigued by the ghostly goings-on the owner and staff alike were wanting some answers.

On the night of Sunday, 22nd January 2006, the team turned up at the property to conduct our all-night investigation. Our good friend and colleague, Tony Liddell, (author of the book *Otherworld North East, Ghosts and*

Hauntings Explored), and one or two guest investigators joined us. We started the evening with a tour of the premises before spitting into two groups to cover the location. The first location for investigation was the upper-floor restaurant. We ventured in and began investigations at 23.15pm. A preliminary baseline test of the room showed no anomalous readings so we then sat down and waited and observed. The room temperature was 23 degrees and, although it was a January night, the humidity levels were quite high. This particular vigil proved a little interesting in the way of minor paranormal activity as one or two disembodied breaths were heard by a few of those present. I thought I saw a black shadow move across the floor from left to right. We were all stationary at this time.

Our team psychic, Suzanne McKay also picked up on a hanging and specified it was related to the building itself and not the area in which we were. The other group at this time were down in the restaurant cellars but they had a slow start to the evening with only a few taps and knocks heard which I dare say could have been the building settling down for the night. Our other team psychic, Glenn Hall, did however pick up on a chubby, grey-haired fellow with a moustache, and said he had a blue apron on. He was given the name Dolan. Could he have been a joiner, or one of the many tradesmen that are known to have worked here? It's a tantalising thought.

We regrouped at 00.15am and had a quick break before heading off to our next locations. It was our turn in the cellars, and it did not disappoint. We were only sitting in the cellar for about a minute or so when I felt a sharp pull on the bottom of my right trouser leg; this was accompanied by a sharp drop in temperature, which adds credibility to the occurrence. The temperature in the room then returned to its original reading of 23 degrees. Our team psychic Suzanne McKay then complained of feeling dizzy and disorientated and said she couldn't - or wouldn't - turn her back on the doorway, for reasons she could not specify. She also picked up on a spirit person called Headley and could not determine if it was a man or woman. Interestingly enough, census records do show that in 1881 a family resided at this residence with a boarder or lodger named Heddon. Could this have been whom Suzanne meant? After all, messages do indeed come through somewhat jumbled and unclear at times. The ambient room temperature at this point then dropped again to 20.7 degrees.

The most interesting results in the cellar were yet to come. While we were calling out to the atmosphere it was noted by team Investigator Darren Olley that a plastic bag hanging up in the cellar was rustling. When he looked to see what the noise was he noticed it was swaying slightly from side to side although there was no one near it at the time. Draughts and breezes were eliminated in our initial baseline recordings. A mist anomaly was then seen in the middle of the room by guest investigator Tony Liddell, and with his naked eye. It was accompanied by a massive drop in both temperature and humidity, but unfortunately the night-vision video cameras we had running at the time failed to record any hard evidence of this mist. This annoyed us all no-end, but that is just how ghost hunting is. Nevertheless - an interesting vigil indeed, which produced some fascinating results.

Onwards to the next location, and this was the entrance foyer and reception area to the restaurant. This vigil proved very quiet indeed in regards to actual, auditory phenomena but the coffee machine and the credit card machine did seem to turn on for no reason and begin functioning. We thought this was odd, but the restaurant staff that joined us on the investigation told us this was quite normal and a rational explanation was found. However, two interesting photographs were taken in this vigil. Both of these photographs were taken by two different investigators using different cameras at different times in the vigil. The anomalies both appear in the same area of the room, showing a similar streak of anomalous light. What they are for sure is still baffling investigators and is proving very interesting within the paranormal research field. At present they are believed to be orbs in movement or spirit paths or doorways into our world called vortices. Until more research is done on these types of phenomena we can't say exactly what they are.

On to our last location in the investigation, which was the downstairs restaurant area. Suzanne McKay almost straight away picks up on a spirit lady called Cynthia Labelle or Label, but research showed no one of that name having worked or resided at this property. Knocks, taps, and what we all thought were footsteps were heard in abundance during this vigil along with a Dictation machine being moved across the top of the counter while no one was near it. It seemed to have occurred while we were all sitting at the opposite end of the room, observing and monitoring the area. Its interesting to note we all heard shuffling and movement coming from the area in which the Dictation machine was placed and, when we went over to take a look, we found the sound-recording device had been moved quite a distance from where it was left. A good result. My night-vision video camera was then trained upon the Dictation machine in the hope it would move again on tape, but alas it did not.

Whilst monitoring this location we had left our infrared beam barriers down in the corridor hoping something may trip the beam while no one was there (as we usually do). I ventured to the top of the downstairs restaurant to take a look down the corridor and, in retrospect, it was probably the best thing I had done that night. As I looked down the corridor I saw one of our guest investigators standing at least five to six feet away from the sensors taking photographs. Suddenly the motion sensor was tripped and the alarms went off. This gave the guest investigator a bit of a fright and he exited the corridor quite quickly. No one was near the sensors when they went off, as I, the guest investigator and another team member can verify. The sensors were left for the rest of the investigation and failed to go off again. In addition to that they were also checked after the investigation, and it has been determined that the batteries were indeed working soundly. So, who tripped the beam?

It is also very interesting to note that Tony Liddell was monitoring the area at the time from the downstairs restaurant and, as before in the cellars, a magnificent temperature drop accompanied this phenomenon. It was also one of the areas that the owner had told us was very active and phenomena had been reported by the staff.

To summarise, the Investigation carried out at the *El Coto* restaurant on 22nd January 2006 was a fascinating one to say the least. The phenomena we recorded during the early hours were very interesting and had the investigators present quite amazed and dumbfounded. Although the investigation was rather slow to begin with, paranormal phenomena did indeed occur and were witnessed and recorded by the majority of investigators attending. Although different types of phenomena were witnessed at different times during the night, fortunately more than one person witnessed them at the same time. This fact alone makes the phenomena all the more credible. It is not often that this happens on investigations and usually there is only the one who bares witness to any alleged phenomena and, as is often the case, they question themselves as to whether it actually happened at all. For this reason the investigation at *El Coto* is one I will always remember. The evidence ascertained is, I believe, very credible and does indeed help to support the theory and the validity of ghosts and hauntings.

The building itself at 21 Leazes Park Road, as mentioned earlier, dates back to the middle 1800s and has seen a lot of people come and go. Used as business properties, retail outlets and private dwellings it would be fair to say the building is haunted as it is steeped - rich in - history. Remember, when ghost hunters investigate buildings and properties, nine times out of ten it is the actual shell of the building that is being investigated, and not the modern-day interior that it houses; in this case a Spanish restaurant.

Chapter Seventeen

Serving Up
Some Spirit Pt 2
The El-Torero
Restaurant,
Newcastle upon Tyne.

The El-Torero Spanish restaurant is located on Newcastle upon Tyne's "Side" that runs down to the quayside behind the Black Gate. The owners of this fine establishment let us in to investigate after we had investigated *El-Coto*, their sister restaurant in the Leazes area of Newcastle, of which the investigation results can be read in the previous chapter of this book. Not much is known about the actual history of the restaurant other than that it was another restaurant prior to that, and - when the building was constructed in 1905 - this particular spot was both a Post Office and a bank. We also know that the actual building it is housed in runs up the Side, and is called Milburn House. The head of the Side was once railway viaducts, which led to the corner of Milburn House. The old viaduct ran straight through where the building is now situated to Amen Corner, which is next to Newcastle's great cathedral.

Milburn House was built with funding from the Milburn family and, because of their connection with shipping; the floors are labelled deck-style with A at the top and G on the ground floor. On 26th September 1748, Admiral Lord Collingwood was born in a house somewhere on this site; but where, exactly, no one is sure. Could he been have born in a house which is now the *El-Torero* restaurant? Could his ghost still wander aimlessly in the place he once called home?

Since the *El-Torero* restaurant began its business at these premises in 2001, the owners and staff have become convinced that it is haunted. On a number of occasions the sense of an invisible presence has been felt by an abundance of staff, leaving them quite on edge to say the least. A lady who once worked there, while on the premises alone, heard her name being called out. Thinking she must not be alone after all she replied to the voice only to get no answer. She stopped what she was doing and promptly had looked around to see who it was. She found that she was indeed alone in the building and all the doors were locked. This phenomenon is often documented during a haunting and is more common than people think. Then there are the sightings of a ghost-lady who is reported by some to have been seen in one of the mirrors in the restaurant.

On the night in question *The North East Ghost In-Spectres* research team arrived to carry out our investigation. We were joined by a few members of another north east-based ghost-hunting team for tonight's investigation. Members of Team Phenomena were on hand to lend assistance. Previous baseline testing showed no anomalous readings anywhere in the building and the room temperatures were what you would expect, so everything was quite normal. We spilt into two groups after the place was vacated and by around midnight on the 13th March 2006, we started the investigation. My group started investigating in the bar area of the restaurant. We placed several sets of motion sensors down in certain areas and a trigger object was drawn around and left. The room temperature measured on average 25 degrees and the humidity of the room was at 55%. We then called out to the atmosphere in the hope we would get a response from any spirits that may have been present. Team psychic Glenn Hall was in my group for these vigils and I asked him what his first impressions were. He told me that he got the feeling of a nearby fire (perhaps in another area of Milburn House). He also felt that people were rushing past through this area to escape the smoke and flames. Further, he sensed burning ash and cinders raining down outside.

At 12.35am we settle down and just observe. Ten minutes go by and nothing happens, so I call out to the atmosphere again - to no avail. The sounds of keys are heard chinking and jangling in the distance but upon inspection we find our host for tonight (staff member Heather) entering the office to access the CCTV system for the other investigators to monitor. We resume our vigil and one of our guest investigators from Team Phenomena decides to try and dowse for communication using the crystal pendulum. At this point Glenn tells me that he feels that a spirit-woman has been seen around the area where the table and mirror are situated. He goes on to say that when people come out of the lavatories they are startled by this vision.

Little did Glenn know that earlier, while I was chatting with staff member Heather, she told me that this is where the spirit of the woman had actually been seen. The crystal pendulum indicated that the spirit of a woman was present. The dowser then felt the area surrounding him going cold, but the laser temperature gun disagreed. The area around him was still 25 degrees and the humidity stayed at a stable at 55%.

The dowsing continues, and the age is 61 is determined. The initials *E* and then *G* are then given and the 1700s were also established as this lady's time of death; but without more information it is hard to determine who this person actually was. This lady also said, via the pendulum, that she would produce some phenomena; alas she did not. The room temperature was now at 21 degrees, but considering the heating system was slowly cooling down this was to be expected. To end this first vigil we tried a small séance around one of the tables. Nothing paranormal happened.

The other group was investigating the kitchen areas of the restaurant and, upon entering the area they registered no EMF or temperature anomalies. This stayed consistent throughout the first vigil. Suzanne McKay feels that these areas are quiet and not subject to hauntings. She is indeed correct, so - after this location was investigated -it was withdrawn from my list of vigil areas for the night's investigation. So far both our team psychics seemed to be producing the goods.

Location Two and we are now investigating the back storerooms and rest areas. It is now 1.20am. Earlier on while the motion sensors were being placed down, two investigators claim to hear the sound of someone shuffling and moving around. They claim to be both motionless yet still hear movement close by. No one else is with them. We venture in to investigate and settle ourselves down; it is not long before one of the Team Phenomena members jumps and cries out in terror as he claims something touched him on the ear. I swap places with him and ask, if that was indeed spirit, could they perhaps touch me in the same way? It did not.

While I was taking photographs along the corridor I did see what I could only describe as thick, wispy smoke, or a mist anomaly when my flashgun went off. It was clear as day and no one present was smoking. (It is our team policy not to smoke on investigations for exactly this reason). To my absolute horror and annoyance it did not show up on my picture, yet I saw it light up in my flash. On with the investigation, and more crystal dowsing is tried only this time to no avail.

We decide to split up for a while, so we all take a small area of the back rooms each. Nothing at all seems to be happening except for a nice light anomaly caught on one investigator's night-vision video camera, so we regroup. So far it seems the back rooms are the active area of the restaurant with light and mist anomalies seen, and with auditory phenomena heard too. We realise this and decide to stay a little longer as break time was looming. Unfortunately, nothing else happened. The other group was investigating the main restaurant area and a tapping noise was heard by all present. They couldn't determine the source but thought it may have been the building settling down. The name Marianne or Anne comes to Suzanne as well as some other evidence. This was exactly right, but unfortunately had to be dismissed for a number of reasons.

The rest of this particular vigil was rather quiet. The motion sensors and trigger objects we had placed down at the start of the investigation had failed to supply us with any results of significance and the rest of the night's investigation, I can safely say, proved rather fruitless to say the least. Things were starting to quieten down. It had not been a bad night and we have concluded that there is definitely something odd going on at the back of the restaurant as this place seemed to be the area for the best results. With a building as beautiful and as old as Milburn House (with the restaurant being only a tiny part of it) you can't be surprised if it is reputed to have a ghost or two.

Chapter Eighteen

The Mystery of the Morgue The Coroners Court, Newcastle Quayside.

As readers will have noticed in chapters 10 and 15, the author is a serving member of another north east - based investigation unit called *Ghosts and Hauntings, Overnight Surveillance Team.* (GHOST)

One thing the GHOST Investigation team is known for in the north east of England is that we try to investigate haunted locations that have never before been done. This property examination is no different. On the night of 24th February 2006 we were due to investigate the Sea night-club on Newcastle quayside, otherwise known as Neptune House. As the nightclub was open late we had to wait until 3.00am before we could get in to conduct our survey. Iron-ically, prior to this particular case study, we were allowed access into the Coroners Court building, which stands adjacent to the Sea club. This venue had also never been investigated prior to the GHOST team going in, and it is this investigation I will elaborate upon now.

This building was constructed in the late 1800s - around 1888 - and was once used as a mausoleum and a morgue. It belongs to the same people as the sea club, is more or less unused except for one room - and that is for administrative and managerial purposes. The team's event organiser Lee Stephenson was told by the property owners that they also felt this building was indeed haunted. Strange occurrences and odd noises have been experienced by some of the staff while in there. An eerie "sense of presence" had been felt and the feelings of being watched had also been reported.

This chapter details the events that happened while the GHOST investigation team were in the Coroner's Court. On the night in question we arrived at the premises at about 11.30pm and immediately set about conducting our baseline tests and setting up our trigger objects. In the old morgue we placed a trigger object of a crucifix. The temperature read 13 degrees and no EMF anomalies were recorded. On the ground floor we placed another trigger object of a crucifix and the temperature read 4.5 degrees and no EMF anomalies were recorded. On the upper floors no trigger object was used, but the room temperature was 3.5 degrees and again no EMF anomalies were detected. It should also be noted that as we were on the Quayside in Newcastle on a Friday night the chance of noise pollution was very high indeed. Great care was taken not to misinterpret any possible auditory phenomena.

We spilt into two groups to cover more of the building. In group one were myself, Lee and Mark Winter (guest). In group two there were Drew Bartley, Fiona Vipond and Rob (guest and staff member). Our group stayed on the middle floor for the first vigil. At 12.55am I photographed my first light orb so I called out into the atmosphere to see if anything would happen. We were not disappointed. A noise resembling a box falling or moving was heard by all present although we were all sitting perfectly still at this point. I then tried to turn on my torch - I had just changed the batteries - but it would not work at all. We found this rather odd indeed.

We then ventured into the other room on the same level where we had placed out motion sensors. As we were standing in the room the motion sensors were tripped and the alarm went off. It has to be stressed that the three investigators were nowhere near the sensors when they went off and further tests proved the batteries were working fine. They did not go off any more that night. A feeling of immense cold around Lee and Marks legs was reported just after the sensors were tripped but this could have been a draught or cold breeze coming up the stairs from the cellars/old morgue. Lee and Mark hold opposing views.

Just at this precise time, Lee caught some nice, moving light anomalies on video camera while the camera was facing the top of the stairs.

We then ventured back into the other room to find our trigger object had been moved about an inch or so of its line. We took photographs of the moved crucifix and ended this first very productive vigil. It didn't take long for us to work out this building had something very odd within its walls. Group two were upstairs and they reported one or two strange noises and unexplained taps, but generally it was a quiet vigil for them.

Our next location saw us in the upper area of this building while the other group staked out the middle or ground floor. Within minutes of starting the vigil at 02.00am two nice, moving light anomalies were caught on video camera. They both seemed to be caught around the loft hatch area on the ceiling. Lee states that there might have been a hanging in this area but subsequent research could not provide any validation.

I call out to the atmosphere and once again Lee catches another orb on the video camera. At this point in the investigation I feel something actually touching the side of my face. It was like walking through cobwebs. I move across the room and it happens again only this time it is on the top of my head. I move around again and once more it feels as though something's touching me.

Was something following me around the room? It certainly felt as if there was. Lee's camera suddenly started to go in and out of focus for a while, which happens quite a lot on investigations and is commonly reported by paranormal investigators all over. By now it was 02.30am and it was the end of a vigil. Team two came back from the downstairs morgue with some interesting results too. Orbs were caught on night vision video camera and unexplained noises were heard coming from by the stairwell. The phenomenon called pulsing also occurred and was witnessed by all down there. This is when a certain part of the room goes even darker and blacker than what is usual and then returns to normal. This happened in the doorway and the light coming down the stairs was completely blacked out for some reason. Was this a trick of the light? Were the investigators' eyes playing tricks on them? Or is it paranormal phenomena?

This pulsing is yet another question that needs answering and more research is needed by paranormal investigators to find out what it actually is. Whatever it is, it's pretty harrowing, as those who have been on paranormal investigations will testify. The group ended their vigil with a séance where, subsequently, Drew's left arm was actually grabbed and squeezed by what he described as an invisible presence.

What will the rest of the night bring? It was our turn down in the morgue now and I was very thrilled about the prospect of this vigil. Little did I know what was actually going to happen. Vigil three started at 02.50am down in the cellar and I started by calling out to the atmosphere. It was jet-black down there and you could not see your hand in front of your face.

At 02.55am we all heard a shuffling noise coming from the top of the stairs that lead into the morgue. I ventured over to the bottom of the stairs and the sounds became clearer. I called out up the stairs to see if anyone was there and got no reply so I climbed the stairs to investigate and, lo and behold, no one was there at all. So what was moving around on the stairs where, earlier on, our motion sensors were tripped? I could find no explanation so I rejoined the group in the morgue, reported my findings and proceeded to call out to the atmosphere. What Lee and myself then heard astounded us both and sent shivers down our spines. We both heard a long drawn out breath, which sound almost like a laugh. This was recorded on videotape. In all honesty though, I do feel it may have been caused by possible revellers that were out on the town but an inspection outside showed no one was there. If there had been, they were now long gone.

I continued to call out and, like the earlier group, we also experienced the pulsing phenomenon in the doorway. The best was now to come as when I was asking and calling out for phenomena, something pulled the clipboard in my hand! I was quite surprised to say the least because this was something physical. I turned on my torch and looked around; the other team members were about three feet away. Reluctantly I turned out my torch and I asked the spirit in the room to do this again and, lo and behold, it felt as though someone tried to pull the damn thing out my hand. It was so hard that my arm was pulled forward. I shone the torch yet again and when I realised no one was near me I knew there and then we had a result. This was the end of the vigil at this location, and what an investigation it was.

The Investigation carried out at this particular venue proved very interesting to say the least. Never before investigated, and unlikely to be investigated again. The Coroners Court, in our opinion had an entity or spirit that roamed the whole premises causing mischief and generally letting people know it resides there. There was nothing untoward or malevolent about it and we think it is that of a male. The similarities between the reported phenomena of the investigation vigils were very striking. Both units heard the guttural breath or laugh, and the pulsing phenomenon was witnessed by both units too. We all witnessed a physical experience, with my clipboard being tugged twice, and Drew's left arm being grabbed.

It's ironic to think that we were supposed to investigate the neighbouring nightclub after it closed to the public at 3am (which we did but returned to the Coroners Court after the results were not so good). It turns out that what we had hoped to do we did not, but subsequently ended up doing something all night we did not expect to. The phrase, *expect the unexpected* springs to mind, and that too is rather ironic.

Chapter Nineteen

One for the Children A Celebrity and Charity Investigation for the Children's Heart Unit Fund

One of the facts not mentioned in this book so far is that a lot of the investigations we carry out are in aid of charity. The charity *The North East Ghost In-Spectres* supports is based at the Freeman Hospital in Newcastle and is called the Children's Heart Unit Fund. It must be emphasized that although they are "charitable investigations" our principles and goals remain the same; to investigate haunted properties. So far, we have conducted a host of investigations for our charity and for this we are immensely proud. This is an investigation report from one of our latest charity investigation nights.

In early April 2006 the biggest charity and celebrity paranormal investigation the north east of England has probably ever seen was held, at Newcastle Keep, for the Children's Heart Unit Fund. Celebrities from the ghost-hunting world, along with two other north east - based research teams, came together with *The North East Ghost In-Spectres* to investigate the ghostly goings on within these ancient castle walls.

Attending the investigation was ITV2's *Haunted Homes* paranormal investigator Mark Webb. Mark was also the paranormal investigator for Living TV's *I'm famous and frightened* and is fast becoming a good friend of *The North East Ghost In-Spectres* research team. They have worked together on a number of occasions.

Diana Jarvis, editor and writer for the spiritual and paranormal monthly publication *Vision* magazine was also in attendance. Accompanying Diana on this visit was York's "Ghost-Finder General" and historian, Rachel lacy. Two north east - based writers and well-known ghost hunters were in attendance too. Mike Hallowell, (patron of *The North East Ghost In-Spectres*), is a freelance broadcaster and writer for *Vision* magazine, and has his own *Bizarre* column in *The Shields Gazette.* Also in attendance was Tony Liddell, author of the book, *Otherworld North East; Ghosts and Hauntings Explored* to lend his expertise. It was indeed an honour to have people such as these at our investigation. The three research teams in question on the night were Team Phenomena, Otherworld North East and of course the host team, *The North East Ghost In-Spectres.*

We arrived at the Keep at 9pm and were let in by the custodian and head warden, Paul McDonald. A brief tour of the castle was then carried out for those who had not visited before, and strict instructions were given to Paul not to give anything away in regards to the hauntings. Diana Jarvis is also a spirit medium, so we did not want her to find anything out prior to the investigation. After collecting in all the sponsor money, the donations, investigation fees, and money donated from Mike Hallowell from the sales of his Native American music CDs; we split up into teams to cover the Keep. In group one there was Diana Jarvis, Mike Hallowell, Glenn Hall, Darren Olley, and myself, and this is the report detailing what happened based on this group's perspective of the investigation. The other groups had very little to report.

At 11.05pm we ventured into our first location which was the Garrison room and Chapel area and placed the motion sensors in the garrison room doorway. The average room temperature was 7.4 degrees, and a prior EMF sweep showed no anomalous readings. A few minutes elapsed and then I asked if anyone was feeling anything or picking anything up. Mike Hallowell told us he was being drawn to the window at the top of the garrison room stairs, outside the condemned cell. Why, he could not say.

Earlier on while the tour was in progress in this area Diana told me that she felt pains in her lower back. Was she picking up on something? At 11.15pm I called out to the atmosphere in the hope of some paranormal activity, I then relocated to the top of the stairs and sat outside the condemned cell. I continued to call out. 11.20pm saw the first of a few decent orbs being photographed in the garrison room. I continued to call out and at 11.25pm we were all pleasantly surprised to hear a loud knock, or bang coming from the corner of the room. Everyone was sitting still and the corner of the room was empty. So what made this noise that came just at the right time of asking?

I came back down the stairs and sat next to Diana Jarvis where we both heard what sounded like a shuffling of footsteps emanating from the dark, dank lower stairwell. Again no one was there. Investigator Darren Olley also heard this noise. Diana then told me she was picking up on a young girl, about 14 or 15 years old, and she had a tooth missing. She had mousey, blonde, dirty, tatty, shoulder-length hair, and she was "scruffy" and "dirty". She was terrified beyond all belief. Diana also specified that she could pick up on her feelings and pick up on what she looked like. She specified this might be residual energy left over and not an actual spiritual presence. The word *ecclesiastical* was picked up around this time by Diana but what it meant she could not say. I thought it might prove to have significance when we ventured into the neighbouring Chapel area.

11.40pm: Darren Olley gets the smell of what can only be described as candles burning, or candle wax. Glenn Hall agrees as he can also detect the same odour. Time was getting on so at 11.40pm we venture next door into the Chapel.

On entering the chapel the temperature measured 7.5 degrees and again no EMF readings were detected. Diana then sensed someone standing behind her in the doorway to the Chapel. Mike Hallowell began to take some photographs' well he tried to but it seemed something did not want Mike to take a photograph as every time he tried to shoot the doorway into the Chapel area, his camera failed to go off. When he turned around and tried to take a picture down into the chapel, the camera took the photo. This happened on 17 occasions and it also happened when others had a go with Mike's camera. What was standing in this doorway? And why did it not want to have its photograph taken? It seems curious that Mike's camera malfunctioned in the area where Diana, and lots of other investigators in the past, have sensed something. On leaving the chapel area Mike's camera worked fine! "Bizarre" to say the least!

At 12.00 midnight the light come on in the castle indicating the end of the first vigil.

On reviewing an EVP recording Mike Made during the course of the first vigil he was astonished to hear a great crash which was recorded while we were all in the Garrison Room. In my opinion it sounded like a cell door slamming, was not heard at the time of the recording and is very interesting to say the least. I also took this opportunity to have a chat with Diana regarding the girl she picked up on while in the old prison. I told her there was a young girl reputed to haunt this room and that she was known as the Poppy Girl. I explained that no one knew if this legend was factual or not as it cannot be historically backed up. I told her my theory about picking up on thought - forms and made - up ghosts if the venue has such a strong and famous legend. She agreed with me saying that you could. It has been done before with a group of investigators who "invented" a ghost, gave him a name, and before long it was producing phenomena! This is a very famous case indeed. She also emphasised that she knew nothing about the castle and its ghosts, and I sincerely believe her. So, whether or not the story is true, she did indeed pick up on *something* whilst down in the bowels of Newcastle Keep.

We started our next vigil at 12.30am and all was quiet in the way of paranormal activity, but Diana Jarvis again impressed us with her mediumship. She picked up on a man with a lantern facing the direction of the river, and the "Lily Marlene" song. For some reason it was going round in her head. The World Wars came to mind and she heard the sound of sirens going off, along with flashes of light coming from outside. Paul McDonald (The castle warden) confirmed after the investigation that the Garrison Room was used as an air-raid shelter, and the fire brigade used the roof as a fire - watching station and actually had sirens positioned on the roof. No one else has ever picked up on this before. Tony Liddell then confirmed that World War II soldiers have also been seen and picked up on within the castle, and I was very impressed with her to say the least. She is very good indeed.

02.00am: We venture into the Great Hall and Diana picks up on the Earl of Strathclyde saying, "I am sorry, I am really sorry." She also picks up on another male spirit but is not sure if the two are connected.

Mike Hallowell then makes another astonishing recording on the EVP machine. While sitting in the Great Hall in silence he recorded the sound of a long, drawn-out breath; two to be precise, one shorter one was recorded just before the other long one. Diana and I both then made a recording with our recording devices and Diana seemed to record some strange noises like a scratching or what sounds to me like a dog sniffing into the microphone!

At 02.20am we then venture into the Kings Chamber. Diane states immediately that she is very uncomfortable indeed and does not like what she is feeling. At this point in the proceedings when I am talking to Diana, I notice she is transfiguring and her face is taking on the form of an older spirit man. This episode lasted for about 20 seconds and every time I looked back at her, the face was still the same. It scared me quite a lot and I nearly ran into the door trying to get away from it. What puzzles and worries Diana is that when a spirit is close or when transfiguration is about to occur, she is fully aware of it.

This time, however, she did not see or feel it coming and this concerned her. Mike Hallowell also caught the end of the transfiguration and he too agreed that her face was "not hers". Diana felt quite ill at this point and we were all now on edge. It must be stressed that I personally did not believe the idea of a spirit form showing itself through somebody's facial features, but after completing 80 Investigations in just over 3 years I have learned that anything is possible. However I do try to keep a rational take on things and the thought crosses my mind that it may have been my eyes playing tricks on me due to fatigue. I guess we will never know for sure.

Mike commented on where he felt the spirit was in the room, and it was in the same place where Diana had transfigured. Mike did not know this as he was out of the room at the time and only came in when he heard the commotion. We then left this area and stood outside the King's Chamber in the Great Hall. Diana stated this spirit was a male spirit after we vacated the room, but I did not say anything about this until after she had mentioned it. So Diana was, again, correct. This episode was absolutely fascinating and I have only seen this type of thing once before out of all the investigations I have taken part in and it really makes me wonder.

Mike Hallowell and Darren Olley then comment on the fact that they feel ice-cold from within while standing in the Chamber. A cold spot is then detected in the doorway leading into the Great Hall and no source could be found for this cold air. The surrounding air measured 4 degrees warmer than the cold spot indicating a possible spirit presence.

Suddenly, and for a brief few seconds, Mike Hallowell starts to tremble, almost as if he was having a minor convulsion of some kind. He said that the entity was getting really annoyed with us and wanted us out. I thought for a moment that he may have been on the verge of being possessed, but he assured us he was fine. The spirit seemed to be "fronting us", trying to get rid of us and was now having a go at Mike. Mike is a good investigator who has been investigating and writing on the paranormal for about 40 years. We decided we should listen to him and leave the vigil early.

After this vigil our last of the evening was in the Galleries, and nothing at all happened. In summary this investigation has to be one of the best investigations to date here at Newcastle Keep. Collectively we have recorded EVPs that cannot be explained, a transfiguration occurred which I personally witnessed, anomalous mists were photographed and auditory phenomena were heard by investigators coming from within the rooms they were sitting in.

On top of that Diana picked up on some amazing facts and details giving us in our group a good show of mediumship. What she picked up on was quite incredible indeed and a lot of what she said can indeed be historically backed up. A plethora of phenomena on what was for me my biggest investigation to date. Biggest in the sense that we had an array of well known people and celebrities with us and the fact that, after all the sponsor money and investigation fees had been collected, and all the donations handed in, we made a grand total of just under £1500 for the Children's Heart Unit Fund in Newcastle. Of that I am immensely proud.

Chapter Twenty

"Can you help me?" (An anonymous Location in Durham City Centre).

Another G.H.O.S.T team investigation and this time we were investigating an old church hall, which is situated in Durham city centre. It is still used as a church hall and community centre today, and it dates back to 1902, which makes it 106 years old. It stands on the opposite side of the road from the church with which it shares the same name (which must remain anonymous due to the nature of this particular building and also at the request of the key holders).

The building in question includes a large hall, a central corridor, two smaller joined congregation rooms and the Parish administrative centre, which was established a few years ago. It is here, at this undisclosed location, that tea and coffee are served after the Parish Communion on Sunday mornings, and it is often used for other public occasions organised by the church and local community. Our visit here was with the sole purpose of a diagnostic examination as no reports whatsoever, as far as we are aware, have come in regarding any ghostly phenomena that may have occurred here.

On the night in question we arrived in Durham city centre for the investigation. The building is quite new in comparison to some of the other venue sites we have investigated in the past, but nevertheless it is still over 100 years old. A lot can happen in 100 years, so we remained hopeful.

When we arrived we set up our base room, which was in the main hall and proceeded to carry out the initial reading of the premises and rooms with *The North East Ghost In-Spectres* and *GHOST* team psychic Suzanne McKay.

The reading began in the main hall and it was here she told us about the spirit of a man whom she felt walks the premises. She told us he was nothing to be afraid of as he was a nice, benevolent soul and was just interested in what we were doing. We moved into the central corridor that runs through the building and she subsequently said that this man had followed us through. At this precise time a moving light anomaly was caught on infrared night vision video camera. She picked nothing else up at this point so we moved into the two back rooms.

In the back rooms it was brought to our attention by Suzanne that a relative of a former priest or vicar had lived in this particular area, as it was once a vicarage. It was *after* the vicarage was used when the relative occupied this living space. The names Alexander came forward and later she sensed a young woman called Murphy.

"Mmm! An Irish connection", I said.

Onwards into the back store room which Suzanne said had once been used as kennels, or somewhere the dogs were kept. Nothing more came to her at that point so we ventured upstairs into the office and we continued with the reading. In here she told us of a male spirit, an authoritative and strict man, and said he had a different energy to that of the man downstairs. The rest of the energy picked up was residual.

Now we had a basic idea of what was what it was time to carry out our preliminary baseline tests throughout the building. A sweep with the EMF meter in all locations showed no anomalous readings and the average temperature of the building was between 22–24 degrees. We placed a number of trigger objects down including a crucifix, the flour tray with a ball in and some batteries, and placed down two sets of beam barriers and motion sensors - one on the staircase and one in the central corridor. We were ready to begin the investigations.

We split in to two groups with Suzanne McKay and myself in group one and Lee Stephenson, Drew Bartley, and Fiona Vipond in group two. Whilst group two investigated the back rooms group one stayed in the main hall. Not a great deal happened with group two in all honesty, except for one or two light anomalies being caught on camera at 1.18am and 1.25am and a cold draught felt at 1.30am. However in our vigil a strong smell of fish was smelt by both Suzanne and myself, and the rustling of paper was heard emanating from the darkness. Inspection found no rational cause for this smell or the auditory phenomena.

A dictation machine that was left recording in this location while we called out for phenomena subsequently left us with no results. But it was at 1.33am when the first visual phenomena came. Whilst I was standing at the table writing my notes, Suzanne saw what she describes as a six-foot black shadow move across the back wall. This gave her something of a fright and she thought it may have been me casting a shadow. Tests proved it was not. Feelings of pains and stiffness down Suzanne's left side led her to think someone in the not –too-distant past may have suffered a heart attack or a stroke in this particular area. Between then and the end of this vigil nothing much else was reported so we re-grouped and had a break.

After the break group one headed off into the back rooms where group two had previously been, and group two headed upstairs to the Parish administrative centre. During this location Suzanne decided to try some rod dowsing but the results were not too good. The rods did indeed indicate a presence; however the information given by the "source" proved rather disappointing. I wondered off into the adjoining storeroom and left Suzanne sitting on the floor. It was not long before we were treated to some fantastic phenomena which I caught on my dictation machine and my video camera. You can clearly hear the sound of what we think was a coin hitting a wall, bouncing off the wooden floor and then rolling for a few seconds before hitting the back wall skirting board. It made some considerable noise and needless to say it surprised both Suzanne and myself. We spent the rest of this vigil trying to work out what had happened. We could not. What we do know is that we picked up auditory paranormal phenomena.

Group twos vigil proved rather interesting with light anomalies being recorded on video camera and a cold, tingling feeling was reported by Drew Bartley on his arm. Not much else happened during this vigil, or so they thought until the EVP machine was played back during the break. What we heard astounded us all beyond belief and it would even send shivers down the spine of the most sceptical people.

Recorded on the EVP machine was a series of unexplained voices, which we can all verify, are not ours! The first voice I believe to be an Irish lady and she is heard saying "CAN YOU HELP ME?"

Oddly enough immediately after this voice you can hear Drew Bartley in the background claiming to have caught an orb on his video camera and it was then he went cold. This woman's voice was not heard at the time! Coincidence? I think not.

The second of these amazing EVP recordings was about 10 minutes after the first when Fiona Vipond was calling out for phenomena. In-between Fiona talking you can clearly hear the sound of a woman in a gentle and loving voice saying "NIGHTIE-NIGHT THEN, THE NIGHT IS OVER".

I think this voice is the same as the first one as this too sounds Irish. The last EVP to be recorded in this vigil appeared about 5 minutes after the second voice and 15 minutes after the first one. It simply said "PICK ME UP".

These sound recordings were recorded by Lee Stephenson's EVP machine and what these voices are and where they come from is still a mystery but many people believe we have recorded the voices of ghosts or earth-bound spirits that are indeed calling out for help, as if trapped between the two worlds. Perhaps we have, but the one thing that was certain on the night was when we heard them for the first time, our blood ran cold! It was a fantastic result. These EVPs can be heard on the GHOST website which can be found at www.ghost-team.co.uk

After the extra long break we had due to listening to these voices and recordings it was group one's turn to spend some time in the room where the recordings had just been made. In all honesty I was quite apprehensive as was Suzanne but nevertheless we ventured up with a positive attitude in the hope we too would get some results. We crept up the stairs ever-so-slowly, half expecting to see the woman in the room when we turned the corner to go onto the room but alas, this did not happen.

We settled down in the office and proceeded with the investigation. Just on the off-chance I decided to leave my audio dictation machine running while in there and in retrospect I am glad I did, as yet another anomalous voice recording was made. I will talk about this recording soon, but first I must point out that the trigger objects that I had previously placed into my flour tray (as mentioned at the beginning of this chapter) had been moved. To be more precise one of the batteries had been pushed over. It must be stressed that we had just looked at the trigger objects when we entered the room and they were just as we had left them. The possibility of the battery just falling over was likely, but highly improbable as they were pushed deep into the flour. It seemed it had been moved while we were in the room.

I turn my attention now to the audio dictation anomalous voice recording. It was not until the day after the investigation when I played my tapes back when I heard what I had recorded.

Suzanne and myself were in the office upstairs and we were calling out to the lady who had recently asked, "Can you help me?" unbeknown to us at the time another voice was recorded and this time it was that of a man. The disturbing thing about this recording is that he says nothing but my name, "Darren!" To hear such an EVP of what we presume is a ghost or spirit is one thing, but to hear one call your name is something else. Now we know there was only the two of us in the room and the other group was investigating another part of the building so the chances of it being one of the other male investigators are impossible. This recording and the other EVPs left us all dumb-founded.

It was now 5am and it was time to call it a night. The only thing that remains to be said is that a second investigation at these premises must be held to find out exactly what is going on. With most paranormal investigations and hauntings you are always left with more questions than answers, and this case study is no different. Who is the lady that is asking for help? Can the historical records show there was indeed an Irish woman who lived or died here, and who is the spirit who called my name? All these questions are being addressed as we speak and, by the time I come to write another book, we may just have some answers.

Afterword

The Word *evidence* as defined in the Oxford English Dictionary is *"a ground for belief or disbelief, matter produced before a law court to prove or disprove a point, to demonstrate"* and is derived from the Latin *evidentem,* which means "clear and obvious" and *evidentia,* which means "proof".

In a court of law, evidence is built up and a case is put forward to either prove or disprove that someone is guilty or not. Without this evidence we cannot convict and neither can we set free, therefore a trial is held to determine the outcome. What I am hoping to achieve within my research is to build up and document the evidence in the hope that one day we can verify and support the theories of the existence of ghosts, and, ultimately, an afterlife.

But how much of the actual evidence in this book that has been presented to the reader will they accept for themselves as proof of ghosts? This poses an interesting question within itself. So what can be defined as *good evidence*? Of course the evidence in a courtroom differs significantly in comparison to the evidence that a paranormal researcher will seek, but essentially, I feel the principle is the same. Until we capture a ghost or an apparition on a 35mm camera, with the added bonus of a negative to back up the picture, or capture a moving ghost on video camera, proving beyond all doubt the true existence of ghosts, we can only gather what evidence we can and present it in an honest way as I feel I have in this book.

Readers must evaluate the evidence we put forward for themselves. Having said that, all experiences are personal to the individual who witnesses them and even when more than one person witnesses the activity, and a joint testimony is given corroborating another's account, still most people refuse to accept this as hard evidence. The team members I have recruited along with the members of other guest teams during my search for the truth are all level headed, respectable personages not prone to overactive imaginations or flights of fancy. They all hold down respectable jobs - for example, nurses, retail managers and even civil servants; most importantly, they all have varied opinions on the paranormal. We are made up of believers and sceptics alike, which I feel gives the team a certain well-needed balance. They are also all very experienced in this field of research.

An inexperienced or novice paranormal investigator may jump to conclusions and become totally irrational due to the fear factor that can take hold on investigations, the mind starts to work overtime, so to speak, and can therefore precipitate the misinterpretation of data so things seem paranormal when in actual fact, they are not. However I feel with my current team and the investigators I work with, we can, at least 99% of the time, discount the possibility of suggestion, anxiety or fear, that comes with frightening investigations; and, when something paranormal does occur, (which quite often it has as you have read) our reaction to this is a lot more objective. This is one way I feel we ascertain *good evidence.* It is also imperative, that

I am able to trust every investigator I work with to give unbiased, honest and reliable accounts of any paranormal activity they may experience on the investigations and to present their written evidence to myself at the end of the night in order for me to compile a thorough report. So, why did I choose these case reports and write-ups for this book?

Since May 2003 I have attended over eighty investigations in more than forty different locations across the north east of England and beyond, ranging from restaurants to rectories, and castles to aeroplane cockpits. Some were interesting, and some were not. At some of the vigil sites we investigated we ascertained very little data, which we feel had no evidential value. However on others we collated a reasonable amount of what we would call good evidence, and this is simply why these particular case write-ups are presented herein. I feel they present and support the best evidential value. I must also stress that we have collated an abundance of video-taped footage of light anomalies, which we consider to be good evidence, and of course we have recorded some good EVP and dictation device anomalies too, and, due to obvious reasons they cannot be included in this book.

Then there is the evidence from the team and guest psychics. "Controversial!" I here you all cry, and yes indeed this is often the case, but when a site is investigated, as in the example of Byker Community Centre, where the history and ghost stories attached to the building cannot be researched prior to the investigation (and I know this to be fact), it does indeed add credibility to the actual haunting and the psychics' testimonies.

Furthermore, the ghostly accounts and odd happenings in the Byker case are from very recent history and are not documented elsewhere, and they are personal to the building staff. This is one case in many where the psychics have proved beyond all doubt that they do indeed have a gift and can communicate with the lost and departed souls as well as "read" the building itself. To me this evidence is irrefutable and goes a long way in supporting the theory of an afterlife and our endless quest for the truth. So I leave you with the evidence that *The North East Ghost In-Spectres* research team has accumulated over the last three years or so. You now hold it in your hands and it is now time for you, the reader to make up your mind.

Glossary of terms

Apparition: The lifelike appearance of a soul or deceased person showing themselves after physical death. (See *ghost*).

Anomaly, anomalous: Something that deviates from the general rule, an inconsistency.

Apport: A solid object that seemingly appears from nowhere. They usually occur in poltergeist cases. They are often teleported from another location.

Astral Body: The image of a body while on an astral journey; some say the soul.

Astral Plane: Believed by some to be another level of existence where the souls move on to after their bodies expire.

Astral Projection: a self-induced out of body experience while in a trance-like state.

Baseline reading: The recording of data such as temperature, electro magnetic fields and humidity etc, prior to an investigation for comparison during an investigation.

Beam Barriers: An infrared beam device with an alarm used in ghost hunting to monitor empty rooms and corridors.

Crisis Apparition: A form of an apparition or astral image projected by a person at a time of crisis, i.e. an accident or at death. A loved one, or close friend usually sees this apparition.

Cold Spot: An area in a haunted location, in which the air temperature measures considerably colder than the surrounding air.

Calling out: To call out to the atmosphere, or any alleged spirits in the location, in the hope they will respond to your request and produce phenomena in order to document.

Control: (To control a vigil location). A course of action undertaken to ensure that the experiments that are being carried out are of the highest possible eminence, therefore ensuring any results established have not been jeopardised by any external influences.

Correlation: An association between two independent witnesses that have experienced the same phenomena, sometimes on different occasions.

Dematerialise: To disappear without trace thereby ceasing to have any material existence.

Disembodied: Lacking a body or freed from any attachment to a body.

Electro-Magnetic Field Meter (EMF): A device in which the natural electromagnetic fields can be measured and monitored.

Electronic Voice Phenomenon (EVP): The recordings of voices and auditory phenomena believed to be from beyond the grave.

Ectoplasm: Believed to be the substance ghosts are made from after being excreted from a mediums body.

Ethereal Body: What the spirit body is said to be made of while on an astral journey or out of body experience.

Ghost: The spirit or soul of a dead person showing

themselves after physical death. (See *apparition* and *spectre*).

Harbinger: A spirit or ghost that is said to be a foreteller of doom or death, often dogs or animals.

Haunt: A ghost that returns to the same place is said to haunt it.

Lock off: A term used in ghost hunting to describe a locked but monitored area or room. Locked to prevent human intervention. Cameras, Dictaphones and trigger objects are normally used.

Medium: A person who claims to be able to communicate with the dead, and relay messages to the living.

Orbs: believed by psychics and mediums to be the first stages in ghost materialization. Round balls of light said to be spiritual energy.

Paranormal: Beyond Normality. Para = Beyond. Above the normal understanding of the natural order.

Psychokinesis: The ability to move objects with the human mind. Recurring spontaneous Psychokinesis (RSPK), is to move objects with the human mind, only being unaware of doing so.

Poltergeist: An old German term for noisy ghost, now termed as Ein Spuk. Nowadays considered being the psychokinetic mind of a troubled or disturbed young individual lashing out frustration without being aware. (RSPK) A psychic temper tantrum.

Pareidolia: Parapsychologists term meaning to find pattern in randomness, i.e. faces in wallpaper, clouds or anomalous mists.

Psychic Breeze: A cold rush of air felt on investigations believed to be spirits passing by.

Possessed: Terms used by mediums indicating their bodies have been taken over by a spirit during attempted communication.

Pick Up: To sense a spirit, to be given a name or a message from a deceased person or from a building.

Residual Energy: The essence of a person left over from bygone days. Energy left over as residue. Apparitions or place memory ghosts are usually residual energy.

Rap - Rapping: To Knock or bang on something in order to communicate. Used by spirits during séances and often in poltergeist cases.

Spirit: The soul of a dead person or a spectral being with free will, and has the ability to move, and communicate.

Spectre: Another term or word for an apparition or ghost.

Sensory Deprivation: A technique or experiment in ghost investigations where one of the senses is deprived in order to enhance the others.

Séance: A method used in an attempt to communicate with the spirit world. The sitters hold hands in a circle around a table and call out to the alleged spirits in order to make contact. It is not recommend unless a trained psychic or medium is present.

Table Tilting: A ghost hunting technique used in Victorian times to communicate with the spirits. Similar to a séance only the spirits lift and tilt up the table in response to questions.

Vortex: A doorway or spirit path into our physical world. Used by spirits to get from one place to another.

Vigil: A designated period of time in a haunted location.

About the Author

Darren W. Ritson is a Civil Servant and lives in North Tyneside with his long-term partner Jayne and their daughter Abbey. He has had an interest in the paranormal for most of his life due to some unexplained happenings he experienced as a child growing up. He founded the *North East Ghost In-Spectres* research team in May 2003 after a lifelong long interest in the subject of ghosts. The team is a non-profit making organization dedicated to trying to find out the truth behind ghosts and hauntings. Ever since he was a small boy he has been fascinated with the thought of ghosts existing, and after experiencing poltergeist activity at the age of thirteen in France in 1986, his path was set and he decided to try to learn more.

Over the next 20 years he built up a library of books, magazines and literature on the paranormal including the works of the late Harry Price (1881-1948) and Peter Underwood FRSA of which these two prolific ghost researches and writers are his main influences. It was then (once he had learned what he would deem sufficient) that he formed his research team. The team at present consists of nine individuals and their goals are simple; to collate data and signed witness testimonies, and to gather evidence from their investigations in order to attempt to piece this elusive paranormal jigsaw together. They try to take a scientific, objective and professional approach to each investigation they undertake, and although they believe in ghosts, each investigation is looked at sceptically.

Evidence collated is viewed and looked at objectively and a process of elimination is carried out before producing findings in a full investigation report. Any good evidence is usually sent for further analysis. Darren is immensely proud of the team he runs and the work they have carried out, and they will continue to investigate, write, and interview witnesses in their endless quest for the truth.

A lot of the work the team carries out is featured in the local newspapers, and the press are always interested in what they are up to and where they are going next. They are fast becoming a well-known and respected research team in the north east of England. It has always been a long-term goal for Darren to write this book and now after all the time he has put in to the team's investigations and the money he has invested from out of his own pocket, it has now been possible for him to compile this book.

Printed in the United Kingdom
by Lightning Source UK Ltd.
115361UKS00001B/227